AMATEUR HOUR

AMATEUR HOUR

Wembley Dreams in Football's Lockdown Era

Johnnie Lowery

pitch

First published by Pitch Publishing, 2025

1

pitch

Pitch Publishing
9 Donnington Park,
85 Birdham Road,
Chichester, West Sussex,
PO20 7AJ
www.pitchpublishing.co.uk
info@pitchpublishing.co.uk

A CIP catalogue record is available for this book
from the British Library.

ISBN 978 1 83680 119 1

Typesetting and origination by Pitch Publishing

MIX
Paper | Supporting
responsible forestry
FSC
www.fsc.org   FSC® C010615

Printed and bound on FSC® certified paper in line with
our continuing commitment to ethical business practices,
sustainability and the environment.

Printed and bound in India by Thomson Press

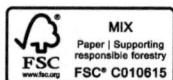

Contents

For Grandad Lowery, who
thought that modern football was
'a load of shite'

Preface

September 2020

THE MAJORITY of the 46,781-strong crowd roar into life as the favourites take the lead after just two minutes, dispelling any early nerves that may be lingering. For a while, it looks as though the underdogs might collapse as the onslaught continues, the bar struck with one effort and the star striker surprisingly off target for a further two good chances. But then, out of nothing, a corner. It's swung in, the keeper comes but gets nowhere near it, and the ball carries on towards the far post. Waiting there is the underdogs' veteran centre-back, the focus of much media attention in the build-up to the match. This is the biggest game of his career, and quite possibly his last. Quite implausibly, he gets to it first and chests the ball goalwards. A corner of the ground erupts; the rest of it looks crestfallen. Still, there's a long way to go and the favourites are still in control, right?

Just over an hour later, the stadium is in a state of shock. That small corner of fans is delirious, and a northern-sounding voice on the commentary is almost in tears of joy. It's 3-1 to the underdogs. There are tears in the other end too. This was not meant to happen, not the end to the fairytale story that was almost inevitably set to unfold. The minutes tick by, but the scoreline does not change, and there's even time for a fourth goal to rub salt into the wounds. For the heavy pre-match favourites, the joy of the first couple of minutes cannot seem any further away. There are even calls for the manager to leave, despite him having guided the side to the league title that year. Meanwhile, the veteran centre-back and goalscorer is paraded as a national hero.

Which game do you think I've described here? A top-level Premier League clash perhaps? Maybe a cup shock, with the likes of Liverpool or Manchester City dumped out by more unfancied opposition, perhaps a Championship side or League One at a push. With either of these theories, you couldn't be much further off the mark.

This was Hereford FC vs Morpeth Town, in the final of the FA Vase at Wembley in 2016. The Bulls were on their way back from liquidation in 2014 as a fan-owned club, and had cruised to the title in the Midland Football League Premier Division. Morpeth were the underdogs, despite being the latest in a series of FA Vase success stories from the Northern League, where they had finished in fourth place, though some way off top spot. The veteran centre-back was 45-year-old Chris Swailes. Just a couple of years earlier, he had been diagnosed with the heart condition atrial fibrillation, needing to be given electric shocks three times after his heart stopped. Swailes retired from playing after the final, a full 24 years after his first FA Vase triumph with Bridlington Town, and who can blame him? It's hard to top a win at Wembley for your final match, especially when you've scored and been named man of the match.

You often hear fans of a non-league club bursting into song about going to Wembley in an FA Cup tie. This is, of course, in jest. There might be the odd shock victory against a League One or Two side along the way, but eventually the Goliaths come in and overpower the brave Davids left hanging on in the competition. By contrast, ditties about Wembley in the FA Vase may well ring true. Each year, two clubs from the ninth tier of English football or below get the chance to run out under the arch and play in front of large crowds to try to bring the prestigious trophy home. Even the rounds before that marvellous stage regularly bring packed crowds into tiny stadiums, creating an incredible atmosphere as each side, each unlikely and unfancied in their own way, goes for that coveted Wembley spot. It really is one for the fantasists, and anyone's village team can afford to dream.

* * *

Of course, things this season aren't going to run quite as smoothly. We're in the middle of a global pandemic, and football is hanging by a thread. League records for clubs at this level for the 2019/20 season were wiped by the decision of the FA to render them null and void after lockdown in the UK brought them to a premature close. In a move that perhaps reflects the particular importance of the FA Vase, a commitment was made to finish the 2019/20 competition, as well as starting that of 2020/21 at the same time. At time of writing, in September 2020, Consett and Hebburn are waiting on their showpiece event as 2019/20 finalists, though no date is currently set. The first qualifying round for the following season's competition is more set in stone – it will begin, barring any further changes to government policy, on Friday, 18 September. We are truly in the middle of unprecedented times.

With crowds capped in line with social distancing rules, and the future of many clubs and indeed the sport itself uncertain at best, you might argue some of the charm of the FA Vase may be lost this year. I prefer to think of it as a flower growing in the midst of nuclear apocalypse: a sign of hope, normality, life returning to a world scarred by the effects of this disease. After all, football has a certain power, perhaps most simply summarised as the ability to put smiles on faces. Should we manage to finish this year's competition as planned, there will certainly be 22 very big smiles on final day. I dare say there will be a smile or two put on my face too, as I travel round the country to follow the competition from its early stages to that big Wembley showcase at the end of it.

Of course, it's not that simple. There's no prospect of a capacity crowd at a Premier League fixture anytime soon, and as it stands, not even the sixth tier can have fans in to see the games. The FA Vase may just be one of the most high-profile competitions available to watch at all this season, if it finishes, of course. There's currently no vaccine, though work is under way, which means no real way out. Threats of a winter second wave loom large, and nobody knows what's around the corner. Being able to go and watch live football in these times is a privilege, and something that I'm sure will be key to my wellbeing, but it could be taken away at any point. It's crucial to try and get on with life as much as you can, but also to have that acceptance that things aren't the same, and won't be for some time. What will it be like watching football in a global pandemic?

1

Durham City vs Thackley AFC

18 September 2020

THE 5AM alarm scythes through me, taunting, reminding me of last week's news. It's only because I've left my phone on a cabinet out of reach of my bed, and with the painful screeching of Coldplay as the sound, that I drag myself out of bed to turn it off.

Before midday, we're up in Middlesbrough, the spiritual home of the Lowery family. Though my entire life has been spent living in London, I'm very much on the fence in the stereotypical 'north vs south' debate. There's been many an argument up at university, the cosmopolitan mixing place of the world, where I've been expected to fight my corner, to back up London and the south against the hordes of dirty northerners and their unintelligible arguments citing horrors such as talking to strangers on public transport. I can't bring myself to do it.

The north to me, specifically the rather unremarkable village of Eaglescliffe, is a happy place. I'm 21 years old now, but the days of running around manically with my brother playing *Star Wars* on my grandparents' estate or getting a light ticking-off for repeatedly volleying a football into someone's car in Preston Park still seem like yesterday. Everyone has a story, and everyone will accept you for yours – well, almost. I remember playing football with one lad who didn't seem to have any mates on the estate. Over many days of bonding with him over a diet of predominantly football, I couldn't figure out for the life of me just why he had been shunned by the rest of the kids around him. That was until I eventually got invited back to his house for dinner, and spotted a Newcastle United shirt hanging on his wall.

This particular visit isn't going to be associated with childish freedom and joy, though. Last week's news. After many years of illness, Grandad has decided to stop his chemotherapy.

The whole world seems as if it is in chemotherapy at the minute, moving at the bare minimum speed required to survive. As if it wasn't already obvious, the journey up the M1 is a stark reminder of the state of play. I can't see the expressions beneath the countless compulsory face masks, but I can't imagine they're awash with optimism and beaming smiles. Even the previously simple task of getting a McDonald's breakfast is now run with almost military-style regimentation:

'Machine order only, please, sir.'

'Stand in the yellow circles while waiting for your order.'

'Don't forget to scan the QR code for track and trace.'

'DON'T BLOODY LEAVE THAT WAY. IT'S A ONE-WAY SYSTEM.'

To cap it all, the breakfast wrap isn't on the now-reduced menu, and I have to make do with a damp bacon roll and a flatbread that seems to contain only the plastic cheese that comes with a kid's My First Kitchen set.

Of course, the Covid-19 pandemic is creating bigger problems than just affecting the McDonald's menu. The purpose of my trip up north is of course for family reasons, but I'm keen to see some football while I'm up there. The Northern League has a charm to it, with several historical old clubs and majestic stadia that would have fallen victim to property developers decades ago in London.

Despite my many family trips up to Teesside, the only football I've seen up there has been my dad's team, Middlesbrough. The matchday experience was always quite something for a young teenage boy. For a start, on the train into town, you had to buy your tickets actually on the train rather than before you got on. This was something I'd never seen before. Despite my constant advice, my dad never did stand very far down one end to try and avoid the £5 fare.

Then there was the pre-match drinking at Gilzeans, where complete strangers would point and laugh at me for drinking a soft drink in a pub rather than a lager. At no point did I go to Gilzeans over the age of 13. There was no furniture in the pub, the official story being that they needed all the space they could get on matchday, but everyone said it was to stop tables and chairs being used as weapons when fights broke out. Walking down to the stadium there was another bar with a haggard old woman standing outside, bellowing 'COME AND SEE THE STRIPPERS' at anyone who dared catch her eye. Many had the knowing look that suggested they'd been in before and found out that she in fact was the stripper. Thankfully, we never did go in ourselves to find out.

The match itself was invariably a limp draw against a side Middlesbrough should have been beating, with the atmosphere one of defeat and decline. I knew only a few of the players: Adam Reach and Richard Smallwood, because they'd become star players in my *Football Manager 2010* Arsenal side, and Nicky Bailey, because he started his career at the club I support, Sutton United. I once annoyed my dad's mate by going on about his non-league roots so much he went beetroot red and told me in no uncertain terms to 'shut the fuck up', before grumbling, 'He'll end up back there, he's so shit, you know.' To be fair to my dad's mate, he wasn't wrong. Nicky Bailey made a hero's return to Sutton in January 2016. Just five years or so after lauding him as my idol at Middlesbrough, I passed out in Sutton's club bar after a drinking competition with the man himself.

One of my more recent trips to the north-east was to see Sutton play, in an FA Trophy fixture away to Spennymoor Town, then of the league below us. We'd actually been knocked out in the previous round, but Bromley's secretary failed to reach the high standards of his club's players and left one of their loanees unregistered. Bromley were kicked out for fielding an ineligible player, and at less than a week's notice we were reinstated. The trouble was, our manager had already booked a holiday for that weekend, so we travelled up there with one of the first-team coaches in charge. With a series of injuries, we made the particularly harsh move of bringing two academy players on the long trip up north with us, and then leaving them on the bench the whole time. Our best player by a country mile was teenage emergency loanee goalkeeper Karlo Ziger from Chelsea, who made a string of excellent saves to keep the score down to 3-0. We cursed the Bromley club secretary all the way home.

Grandad is much happier now he's stopped his chemo, and for a good few hours the idea of football leaves my head completely. His life must have been hell for the last few months, the side-effects of treatment combining with the social isolation that lockdown naturally brings. Beaming, he tells us of his plans to finally go out again next Friday, showing the enthusiasm of a student drowning in the delirium of their first week of proper partying. It might only be a trip to the Blytheholme Social Club in Stockton, but I genuinely share that enthusiasm for him. To be honest, I'm amazed at how stoically the man has dealt with everything over the last few years; always the stiff upper lip and the warm smile, whatever may be going on in the background.

He's not a football man, Grandad, but he always entertains it, whether from myself or my dad. A few years back, he even allowed himself to be dragged down to watch my beloved Sutton United at home to Boreham Wood on a cold and miserable Tuesday night in November, the only goal coming as the wind carried a corner over the line without anyone else getting anywhere near the ball. To honour his commitment, I moved away from my usual terrace spot to sit in the main stand with him for the only time in ten years of supporting Sutton.

'What time are you leaving tonight, Johnnie?' breaks me from my trance. Not content with just sitting and talking, my dad and I have been put to work painting Grandad's fence, which is as old as the house itself, a badly kept secret really, looking at it. Despite being hopeless at anything practical, I'd gotten myself into the zone: an artist, the fence my canvas. Splashes of orange therapeutically covering up the age-old blemishes, I can drift off to a world pre-coronavirus, pre-cancer, pre-whatever is bothering me. The words from my dad, who I didn't even realise had gone off for a break, bring me back round again. In a couple of hours' time, I can take a slightly different style of break from the trials and tribulations of life – a trip to watch Durham City vs Thackley in the FA Vase.

The train journey into Durham is notable for a classic ticket inspector vs pissed teenagers encounter. If you ask me, some ticket inspectors really do bring it upon themselves. This guy clearly gets a buzz out of catching people out: the 'Oh, unfortunately, you seem to be sitting in the wrong seat, sir. That's a £1,000 fine' while sporting a manic grin type. This time, it looks like easier pickings for him. A group of lads, well endowed in aftershave and misplaced confidence, are on the train without tickets. You can see the excitement in the inspector reach boiling point as he mentally calculates how much fine money he'll be getting, as if he's on commission and can treat the wife and kids to a new toaster or something equally dull.

But it's not game over, not yet. First, the teenagers pretend to have each other's tickets. This is a classic but is hardly going to work on such an experienced busybody, no chance. There's more to come, though. First, they claim not a single one of them has a card on them to pay, despite the fact they're clearly heading out into town. 'Well then, you can pay later, when the fine doubles,' offers the inspector, that grin returning as he senses he's won. 'Names and addresses, please.'

'Last name Oxbig, first name Mike,' replies one of the group without a second's hesitation. It takes the inspector a bit longer, but the smile's been wiped out as his face burns red. The others follow with perfectly rehearsed fake names, and even a couple of fake addresses for good measure. The kid masquerading as Mr Oxbig has even invested in a fake ID for his alias. As the rest of the carriage looks to hold back its sniggers, the inspector knows he is beaten and makes a hasty exit to look for some softer targets. As the teenagers sit crying with laughter, I can't help but crack a triumphant smile on their behalf.

Durham is a place I'm well acquainted with, and I still honestly can't decide if I love or hate it. Rolling in on the train over the viaduct and glancing out the window, the idyllic scenery never fails to catch the eye. The cathedral takes centre stage, perched majestically on one of the many hills of which the place is comprised, but everywhere you look is a work of art. From the splendour of the cobbled streets to the serenity of the Wear winding through the centre, you might argue the beauty of the place is uncharacteristic of the north-east. But it isn't just the look of the place that's out of character; in fact, the whole city feels almost an affront to the region.

Durham, in its simplest terms, is a student area, and having graduated a few months ago I'm already well into the stage of hating students. Yes, it's jealousy, but the way they stroll around with no real regard for the locals or the local area irks me somewhat. Exeter University has given its host town the reputation of 'Surrey-on-Sea' due to the hordes of middle-class mummy's boys and girls who attend there, and Durham is probably even worse. In the darkest days, otherwise known as term time, you can't go into a pub for fear of hearing about somebody's 'gap yah' or a family dispute centred around the fact Daddy only bought some spoilt brat a Fiat 500 instead of a Mercedes Benz. In 2017, Durham University hit the news when the rugby club held a 'miners' strike' event, imploring students to dress as either miners or Margaret Thatcher's government, with the Facebook invitation reading, 'We want flat caps, filth... a few working-class-beating-bobbies wouldn't go amiss.' It genuinely amazes and, to be honest, slightly disappoints me that more of these pricks don't get set upon by the locals.

It's early in the student year, but there's no shortage of them around as I get off the train. You can tell who they are more often than not by the clothes and makeup they're wearing, and failing that, definitely the accent. One girl staggers along a steep cobbled street in ridiculous high heels, mascara running down her face, smoking a cigarette with a look on her face that reads, 'Oh God; the north is, like, sooooo disgusting.' I try to shoot her back a 'Shut up moaning and get a proper job' look that I've been briefly developing, but it still needs work, and I hope she doesn't mistake it for flirting as I move swiftly in the opposite direction.

For all my criticism, I have to admit I always enjoyed my visits to Durham to visit mates who are studying there. The college bars are exclusive to students, but this doesn't really bother you when it's barely over a pound a pint and there's a pretty girl sat in the corner you can talk to. And then there are the nightclubs. I spent three years at university in Coventry, and not a single night out came close to the ones in Durham. Something seemed to happen every single time

I visited; my personal favourite being having to drag a mate away from the Evensong event at Durham Cathedral, as someone else had previously told him this was an 'evening gathering of people to piss' and he had suddenly become quite desperate to relieve himself. Luckily, we made it to the morning without a future court order to worry about.

On this occasion, however, there is no real time to reminisce, as Durham City do not actually play in Durham. Instead, I have to jump on a bus to the nearby village of Willington.

Willington is certainly not a student area; indeed, it is hard to think of anywhere more different to Durham, despite the 20-minute bus journey between the two locations. The former lifeblood of the village in the colliery now lies hidden, covered by dust and earth, almost like a dirty secret. Much of the rest of the village is frozen in time, rugged but homely. Like many other similar County Durham villages, Willington is a former pit town, and sprang up rapidly in the late 1800s as Brancepeth Colliery became a site of increased economic value. Migrants travelled en masse from Ireland and Cornwall, as famine and the failure of tin mines respectively left people seeking a new life. Conditions were poor, and the owners of the mine were said to have treated workers incredibly harshly. The evidence, an indelible mark on the history of the village, can be seen in the village churchyard which contains the graves of many of the 162 men and boys who died working there. One disaster in 1896 killed 20 in one blast, the youngest just 14 years old.

There are more upbeat elements to the history of the village too, and certainly significant ones. The Rocking

Strike of 1863, in which miners protested against the mine owners not following new payment rules, is widely believed to be the first time coalminers ever laid down their tools in protest. The strike started in late October and lasted for over two months, before a series of evictions forced the miners back to work in order to survive. Many went through incredible hardship, with starvation not uncommon, in a move that helped lay the groundwork for future trade union movements.

The football ground itself has its own history, harking back to a now bygone era. Willington AFC were generally successful in the interwar period, but it was not until after the Second World War had subsided that they had their greatest success. The legacy of an FA Amateur Cup win in 1950 can still be seen today: the main stand at the ground was built from the proceeds of defeating Bishop Auckland 4-0 at Wembley in front of a crowd of 88,000. Situated right in the middle of the village, the ground has been scaled back in recent years, but it is easy to see just how large it would have been back in that era. Indeed, a crowd of 10,000 turned up at Hall Lane to see Willington play Bromley back in 1953. The large grass banks behind the goals cover up where large cinder terraces used to lie, enabling that large crowd to pile in back before health and safety was such a concern, or even considered at all. I somewhat doubt that much space will be needed for the Durham City game tonight.

To describe Durham City's recent history as volatile would be an understatement along the lines of describing the Cuban Missile Crisis as a simple miscommunication. Things were looking bright back in 2009 as the Citizens won promotion to the Northern Premier League Premier Division, the highest level they had played at since their Football League days of the 1920s. With significant financial backing, the plan was to keep the club moving up the pyramid, perhaps returning those Football League glory days and bringing them in line with the likes of Hartlepool and Darlington. However, their business model included playing on an artificial pitch, which had been installed in 2006 as plans to climb the football pyramid were about to come to fruition. This fell apart very quickly when the Football Conference, the next promotion up from the Northern Premier League, turned around and said artificial pitches would not be permitted in their league.

Deeming this as too much of a stumbling block to any hopes of further progression, the main sponsor behind the club pulled out immediately. The achievement of playing in the Northern Premier League quickly turned into farce, as Durham had to draft multiple academy players and students in to fulfil fixtures. With results along the way including a 10-0 hammering at Boston United and three 7-0 home defeats, they finished the season with a grand total of 0 points and a goal difference of -141. They did briefly stabilise in the division below, but after two years they decided to resign for financial reasons and dropped back into the Northern League, where the brief journey into potential glory had started.

At this point, though, the problems had only just begun. Former Newcastle United favourite Olivier Bernard bought the club in 2013, promising big things, including producing players for the England squad. Instead, a dispute with the landlords of their New Ferens Park ground saw Durham made homeless in 2015, with relegation to the tenth tier of English football following a year later. Things got progressively worse still as they finished bottom of this division in 2019 and had amassed just eight points when the 2019/20 season was suspended due to the Covid-19 pandemic in March. Their opponents for this FA Vase tie, Bradford-based Thackley AFC, could not be more of an antithesis to Durham – they have played in the same division since 1982.

The keen demographist, or anyone with any observational skills whatsoever, would note something slightly unique about the Durham side that lines up tonight. A quick glance at the 2011 census shows 96.6 per cent of County Durham's population is white, a figure that rises to 99 per cent in the Willington ward. However, Durham line up with just one white player in the starting XI, a highly cosmopolitan line-up for the Northern League.

Durham, in their fantastic red and black crossed shirts, are the underdogs for sure tonight, and confidence doesn't seem high among the locals.

'Who do you think's going to win, Daddy?'

'I think the blue team, 3-0, son.'

The game kicks off a couple of minutes late, owing to the fact the penalty spot needs painting on properly, and I find myself quickly getting into supporting the home side. They look clearly second-best in all aspects, but a couple of early chances on the break give a degree of hope to the 100 or so home supporters scattered around the ground. Four league games into the season, Durham have lost all four yet are somehow still the league's top scorers. It's easy to see why, too, as they seem to favour attacking flair over defensive solidity, making for an exciting match.

They're the classic underdog in more ways than one, as the players look almost a bunch of misfits. The central midfielder has a gut that betrays his level, while several of the players look to not even be old enough to be out of school. The match programme bemoans the lack of 18 absent players, mostly through injury, but also including one who has just left and moved to Andorra to seek Champions League football. Yes, really.

Thackley, by contrast, seem to fit the role of pantomime villain very well. Immaculately drilled and looking professional throughout, they are well trained in the dark arts, knowing when to stay down for a few seconds longer than needed, or when to surround the ref if a decision is slightly controversial. The young Durham right-back, who doesn't look older than about 16, is the main target of their protests after two fouls inside the first ten minutes. The quickest the Thackley number six runs all game is up to the referee to demand a card after the second one. Thankfully, the referee holds off, but there is a reason the fouls keep coming from the home side. They simply can't keep pace with the visitors; there's a clear gulf in class just waiting to become more evident.

The resistance is finally broken after 25 minutes and ended altogether when Thackley get a second goal five minutes later. The way the second comes about aligns perfectly with the reputation I've created in my head for the visitors, as there is more than a hint of controversy about it. A recovering Durham player is tripped off the ball as the Thackley winger surges forward, leaving them a man short at the back. The ball is squared, and midfielder Seb Scaroni is able to walk it in after rounding the keeper, a goal which looks to be almost taking the piss. I'm furious, despite only having been supporting Durham for half an hour, and join the accusations towards the ref of being a cheat, a wanker, and far worse.

It doesn't get any better for the home side. The brief chances they'd had on the counter are now drying up. The Thackley centre-back, now with little to actually do in terms of defending, refocuses his energy from shouting at the ref to giving all the generic clichéd encouragements to his team-mates doing all the work. 'Still 0-0, lads, let's keep going, BLUE HEAD,' all while being at least 30 yards from any action. He gets a shooting opportunity at one point, though, clearly bored of staying back, but the effort poses more danger to a black and white cat perched on the grass bank behind the goal than it does to the Durham net. The shot barely misses the cat, but it seems unperturbed, staring back as if daring them to have another go. Instead, Thackley make it 3-0 before half-time.

With the game now over as a contest, my mind wanders to other matters. How far away are the toilets from where I'm standing? How can the bus company get away with charging £4.80 for a 20-minute journey when it's less than a third of that in London? Has anyone ever spent a full 24 hours in a 24-hour Tesco? Sadly, the answer to the first of these questions is about as far as physically possible, so I have little time to ponder the economics of north-east public transport or the endurance of supermarket shoppers as I head towards the clubhouse. As I stand at the urinal, something quite bizarre for somebody from London happens. The bloke pissing in the urinal next to me starts talking to me. What do I do? I'm not used to this at all. Luckily, all he's doing is moaning about the performance, and there's plenty to go by on that particular topic. 'Aye,' he agrees with one of my comments, 'and they were shite at Easington last week too.'

With this slightly odd conversation over, I head off in the opposite direction out of the toilets to find a new vantage point for the second half. Only two Durham fans stand behind the goal their side are due to attack, with the vast majority leaning towards the Thackley end. I can't help but admire the optimism of those two fans, as the action is almost certainly going to largely be concentrated a good distance away from them in the second half. It's not an optimism I share, and I reluctantly move around to join the crowds down towards the other goal. At least the cat should be safe now.

It's not uncommon at non-league football for a cloud of steam to rise from the direction of the tea hut as the ovens are put out, so when I notice some haziness five minutes into the second half I think nothing of it. Weirdly, though, I glance back over a couple of minutes later and it's still there. Then I spot the fire.

Great orange flames lick up the back garden of one of the houses that backs on to the ground, and people start to watch that rather than the game.

The smoke gets thicker as the fire gets angrier, and I find myself coughing and it gets into my lungs. The players, though, get on with the game as though nothing is happening. I hope everyone's OK. It doesn't look good.

After five more minutes of watching the fire, the Chinese whispers reach my section of the ground, and it's good news. The fire is not a house fire, but a large bonfire. The angle of the fence means it's hard to tell this, and all we can see on the far side is the flickers of flame and evil clouds of black smoke floating in our direction. These reports from the other side help me settle down and watch what's left of the game, though the smoke still continues to rise in plumes into the night sky. Quite as to why this household has opted to light a massive bonfire on a Friday night is anyone's guess. Perhaps they've been inspired by the recent Dennis Nilsen documentary and have finally got round to burning all the human remains underneath their kitchen floor. Whatever the reason, it doesn't make for great viewing conditions for those downwind of it.

There's little to report in terms of on-pitch action. The mouthy defender is now screaming 'relax' at regular intervals to try and help his team, in possibly the least relaxing tone I've ever heard. It works, though, and his side get a fourth and final goal with ten minutes to go. The lone Durham striker collapses to the ground as this goes in; the reaction you would expect from a player whose side have just conceded a stoppage-time goal in a cup final rather than a goal that does nothing but embellish the scoreline. As the crowd start to file out, and the bloke next to me hurriedly tries to do a headcount before they leave, Durham finally get a good chance. The left-back, a rare bright spark in a poor performance, runs past three defenders and finds himself in on goal. Sadly, he looks as surprised as anyone at the ease of what has just happened, and his shot is scuffed at the goalkeeper, who could throw a towel over the ball. Shortly after, the full-time whistle puts Durham out of their misery.

After the game, I have the pleasure of talking to the Durham City manager, the former Celtic man Didier Agathe. Make no mistake – Agathe is a big-name manager even at a ground that has seen Malcolm Allison briefly take the reins at Willington in 1984. Agathe's career highlights of a 2003 UEFA Cup Final appearance and a man-of-the-match performance against Barcelona the following year seem a far cry from the surroundings here. So, what was it that made him come over from his home island of Réunion to take the job?

He explained, 'It was good to come to learn and improve myself before going on to bigger clubs. I don't want to go to higher clubs before this experience, so that's why I came here. I don't know a lot about the FA Vase, but I know the final is at Wembley. It's obviously exciting to play these games. I hate losing games, but I'm more concerned now to find my full squad.'

He's incredibly humble; the first thing he says to me is a thank you for taking the time to come and watch his side play. As we stand and chat, the recurring theme is frustration over injuries and absentees, and there is still a hope that his side can climb the table and have a strong season. As I leave the ground and walk across the estate back to the bus stop, I can't help but hope they go on to have a good season too.

Three weeks later, with his side still rooted to the bottom of the table, Agathe leaves his job at Durham City.

2

Whitley Bay vs Newcastle University

19 September 2020

THE BEAUTY of the early rounds of the FA Vase for the obsessives is that you can always find multiple games to go to in one weekend. I'm doing it, of course, but it almost feels against my better judgement. I'm up early, too early, to make sure I can spend some time with Grandad again before I go. Plus, the fence painting needs finishing off. He tells us not to worry too much, that he'll finish it if he needs to, but we both know this isn't going to happen and don't want to leave it half done. It really doesn't help that my old man insisted on us going to the hotel bar before bed last night. I've barely recovered from last week's hangover and certainly haven't caught up on my sleep. He even bought a 12-pack of San Miguel while I was at the Durham game, in case the bar shut before we got down there. By the time I eventually get out to go to the football, it feels like the end of the day rather than the start.

It wouldn't be possible to write about the FA Vase without going to Whitley Bay. The Tyneside club are the most successful in the competition's history, winning the trophy four times since it began in 1974. Even more impressively, three of these wins were in consecutive years. Between 2009 and 2011, Whitley Bay became invincible in the competition, and ultimately went an incredible 27 games unbeaten before finally falling 2-1 at home to West Auckland in the fifth round of the 2011/12 tournament. Paul Chow and Lee Kerr in particular wrote their names into the history books, with both scoring in all three of the final wins. Not content with just this, the 6-1 success over Wroxham in the 2010 final set the record for the biggest margin of victory in the final of the competition. What's more, the opening goal came just 21 seconds in – a Wembley record until Christian Eriksen took just 11 seconds to beat David de Gea in one of Tottenham's league matches at the national stadium. The Bay had also won the FA Vase back in 2002, their opponents in the two-legged semi-final being none other than Durham City.

Success has dried up in the last few years, though. Indeed, the last couple of seasons have seen Whitley Bay fall in the qualifying rounds, ties they didn't even have to play in their glory years. February 2019 saw them fall to their record defeat, a 9-0 hammering at home to Hebburn Town, the ninth goal scored by none other than returning Wembley hero Paul Chow. It had taken them just four months to break their previous record after an 8-0 defeat at Dunston UTS in the same season, in which they finished a below-par 13th.

Expectations are slightly higher today, though, as Whitley Bay face a side from Newcastle University. At Warwick, where I studied, there was a reason the sports teams stuck to Wednesday afternoon games. You simply would not have been able to raise a team on a Saturday. Whether it was a trip to Kinky at Kasbah or Jaegermonster at Neon, neither would involve getting back before 4am or laying off the drink at all. I wonder if maybe this Newcastle Uni side are a bunch of world-beaters, held back only by the fact they're students and thus almost by law have to be out on the town before the weekend's fixture. I hope for Whitley Bay's sake it's been a particularly lively freshers' week, despite the pandemic.

The football that was played at my university could not have been any more at odds with the stereotype of the Northern League. The first XI were encouraged to play a neat passing style on their artificial pitch, carried predominantly by the European exchange students, who had far greater acumen in this department. Even the hopeless society teams in the Wednesday social league generally looked to play the sort of tiki-taka game you don't really see in the English lower leagues. It never worked, of course, but at least in the social league everyone was equally terrible. The games rarely had referees, which meant some of the rough and tumble of the Northern League was replicated in the mass brawls that regularly broke out. In my final year of playing, I'd somehow managed to get sent off in one of those referee-less games, a story I'm always quick to tell when chatting to anybody from north of Watford.

While Durham is only a short jaunt on the train, Whitley Bay via Newcastle is a rather more painful journey. The extra 15 minutes or so on that initial train inevitably lead to me being desperate for a piss by the time we get into the station, but at least I get a chance to briefly take my face mask off before the next leg of my journey. Unfortunately, I make the mistake of doing so in front of the mirror. My face is red, unhealthy, suffering from the perspiration stuck beneath the thin layer of cloth. It's an everyday reminder of what a pain in the arse this pandemic is. In fact, it's such an inconsequential thing to notice in the middle of such a global nightmare sequence of events that I can't help but crack a bitter smile at the grotesque reflection in the mirror. The bloke minding his own business washing his hands next to me must think I'm mad. To be honest, I don't think I'd argue with him.

The next leg is hardly a barrel of laughs, either, with the Newcastle Metro reminding me a little too much of the London Underground. I hate the London Underground. Every single time you take the escalator down to the platform and on to a train, it's like entering a furnace, the depths of hell themselves embracing you. The short trip on the Victoria line on Friday night when coming home from uni feels longer than the train journey up to Coventry itself as you sweat out of places you didn't even know existed. Having made such an effort to avoid it for so long, even the comparatively benign Newcastle Metro brings out a shudder in me as I descend the steps to the misery of the underground platform.

It's reassuring that despite everything that's going on, some things in non-league football will never change. Two kids wearing CP Company goggle jackets and goggle hats eye me up as I step off the train, clones of the teenage 'firms' at every lower-league side in the country. There's looking the part and then there's trying too hard, and these two are very much the wrong side of the line on this occasion. Suppressing a snigger, I walk on through the village of Monkseaton on to Hillheads Park, the home of Whitley Bay FC.

One of the great long-held student traditions is the 'dirty pint'. A classic initiation for the youngsters, it involves a mix of various types of alcohol if you're lucky, and various types of general substances if you're not. If there were any Newcastle University students still needing to complete this initiation, they could have avoided a lot of hassle in mixing the drink by simply ordering a pint of Foster's from the bar at Whitley Bay's ground. It's obvious they either haven't changed the barrel since the bar was last open back in March or haven't cleaned the pipes in significantly longer than that. I suspect it's probably both. One of the other three people in there goes up to the bar to complain, leaving me to ponder over my own course of action. Complaining isn't really a very British thing to do, and I am already taking liberties by charging my phone at a socket on a stage that is clearly labelled with several signs instructing people to stay off it. Instead, I decide to show my disgust by not ordering another pint and heading out to take a look round the ground half an hour before kick-off.

Hillheads Park wouldn't look out of place hosting football several tiers above the level it does. All round the stadium is terraced, giving plenty of room for the supporters to voice their support or indeed frustrations. The old-school main stand dominates the near side, though social distancing regulations mean there aren't many people in it today. Despite its impressive size, it's dwarfed by the Whitley Bay Ice Rink in the background, a rather novel addition to the landscape. If you were to head slightly further down the hill, you would encounter the cricket and rugby clubs too, so the area is clearly a bit of a sporting hub. It seems a bit strange then that the triangle between these three different sports grounds is taken up by allotments. I would have thought Doris would get slightly annoyed at turning up every other week to find a football or cricket ball has smashed through the thin glass of her greenhouse again, but judging by the sheer size of the place, they've obviously put a lot of faith in the accuracy of Whitley Bay's shooting, as anything over the netting would be sure to hit something. The finishing in the warm-up doesn't exactly inspire confidence.

The home side have had a tough start to the season, to be fair, and not as a result of performances on the pitch. A positive test for coronavirus in the camp forced the whole squad into self-isolation for two weeks, with all fixtures postponed. While Newcastle University have played four league games, Whitley Bay have managed just one, a 2-1 victory on Wednesday night away at Bishop Auckland. With an unchanged side today, fatigue could well be an issue and give the students hope of a shock victory. For all their coronavirus-related problems, the Bay also managed to get a good bit of luck. Just after coming out of isolation, a player from their FA Cup opponents Dunston UTS tested positive himself. This forced Dunston to forfeit the tie, putting Whitley Bay through to a big game at home to higher-ranked Witton Albion in the next round. Really, all this messing about does is remind me of the cloud hanging over the season, the threat that all this might be for nothing and the campaign may never make it to a close.

The students probably don't care quite so much, though, so long as there's a night out in there somewhere. They play like a side without any cares, that's for sure, and Whitley Bay don't really get the early foothold in the game everyone there expects them to. You can feel the nerves slowly creep in with each second that the university side stay on top, and then shoot up to a full panic when they take the lead after eight minutes. There are very strong suspicions of offside, but the shouts towards the linesman on the near side are strangely reserved. Perhaps this is because it is, in fact, a lineswoman today. The old bloke next to me instead screams at the referee, while the beaten defenders launch abuse at each other rather than any of the officials at all. Maybe this is coincidence, but it seems a very 2020 form of sexism to me. In my book, all linesmen and lineswomen, regardless of how good they actually are, should receive the same barrage of abuse when making a call against a partisan home crowd.

Luckily, the referee gets himself back onside almost immediately with a soft penalty for the home team. The big left-back, Jamie Dunn, steps up and takes a spot-kick fitting of his appearance, hammering the ball into the net as if he was trying to kill the person stood directly behind it. Had the keeper got a hand to it, he may well have regretted it for the best part of a few months. The panic of five minutes ago starts to ease, and Whitley Bay begin to dominate as expected. You can actually hear the conversation on the terraces start to flow more smoothly, with the majority of the 254-strong crowd becoming more relaxed, more confident the result will take care of itself. Some reasonably attractive girls sitting together in the main stand look less impressed. I assume they are the university football version of WAGs: non-league football isn't typically a hotspot for anyone young or attractive, never mind university girls. There are a few other lads around university age sat in the stand too, keeping the subs that have to sit there due to social distancing regulations company. None of the student supporters make any attempt to mix with the regulars in the crowd. The two groups of fans are simply worlds apart; it's like bringing a knitting club to a Metallica concert. As the old blokes backing Whitley Bay kick every ball along with the players, the youngsters chatting away in their designer gear seem much more at ease. Having repeatedly driven my blood pressure to dangerously high levels watching Sutton, I envy them somewhat.

As with the Durham situation, I find myself leaning with jealousy against the students now I myself have graduated, so I'm as incredulous as everyone else in the ground when the Whitley Bay defender and keeper leave the ball to each other, allowing the student side to once again take the lead. With the fans around me still reeling from this disaster, Newcastle University put a deep free kick into the box. Once again, the Whitley Bay defence forget they're not on furlough any more and leave the student centre-back with a free header at the far post. It's 3-1 to Newcastle University.

'Fucking hell, Whitley Bay, this is embarrassing,' is one of the nicer comments made as the Newcastle celebrations erupt. While they were a bit muted after the first few goals, they really go for it this time, seemingly only just starting to believe that this would-be shock is possible. To put it into context, when the two sides faced each other in the

Northumberland Senior Cup in October 2019, Whitley Bay were reportedly unlucky to only win 6-0, and that was having rested several senior players and indeed just a few days before a 5-1 battering at the hands of West Auckland. The most successful side in FA Vase history losing at home to a team of students really would be a big upset, and this isn't lost on those in red, celebrating like they've just been given the week off lectures. There are no boos at half-time, but a silence that cuts into the air far worse than any shouts of discontent ever could. The tea lady even forgets to charge me for my hot dog, such is her state of anger, briefly cracking a grateful smile when I remind her, before going back to cursing Bay's lack of midfield steel under her breath.

Right on cue, the clouds roll over Hillheads Park, ominous and threatening. Whitley Bay make a change, bringing on experienced striker Scott Jasper, but the home fans aren't exactly enthused by the move. In fairness, it's hard to imagine them being enthused at all by anything other than a full comeback, and that looks about as likely as my previous naive hopes of playing for my university first XI. Jasper is a motivator, egging his team-mates on, but even the half-chances his side were having have now dried up. One gentleman behind the goal tells the Newcastle University keeper, 'This is men's football now, not that student bollocks any more,' which seems a weird comment to make at a side playing you off the park. Nobody laughs; nobody even smiles. Most of the crowd behind the goal seem to have resigned themselves at this point. The rest soon follow when the students make it 4-1 on the hour mark.

Despite bizarrely putting their left-back up top as an emergency striker, there's no way back from here for

Whitley Bay. There's still time for one more odd shout, though, and this time from their own keeper, who tells his side to 'stop fucking things up' with little over ten minutes to go. It's nice somebody has finally shut the stable door, but the horse has already bolted and wandered on to the A19 to be hit by a speeding articulated lorry this time, I'm afraid, mate. Walking round to the exit a few minutes before time, the inquest has clearly already started, judging by the snippets of conversation I overhear. Theories range from the players being tired after the midweek game to being very complacent or simply to being 'too shit', as one particularly unimpressed old bloke puts it. As an announcement tells fans to pick up their FA Cup tickets for next week, there's a frustrated groan and lament of, 'I wish I could cancel them fucking FA Cup tickets.' I certainly hope he didn't. Three days later, Whitley Bay shock Witton Albion, two divisions above them in the football pyramid, beating them 3-2.

Newcastle University understandably look delighted at the full-time whistle, but I don't hang about today to share in their celebrations. Certainly, they deserve their win, and it is a great story, but I have other places to be. Racing back to the Metro station and on to the train back to Darlington shaves valuable time off the wait for steak-and-cans-of-lager night at the northern Lowery household. The evening does not disappoint. I've always felt time flies by watching football. It's what I tend to look forward to all week, but the football is running-in-treacle stuff compared to this. After tracing a family tree back countless generations, Grandad regales us with tales of his days as an international darts player, by which he means playing darts in every country he lived in. In fairness, it's not a short list. After a few beers, everyone watching the darts on the TV reckons they could be a successful international too, without any desire to ever prove this, of course. Quit while you're ahead, and failing that at least before you're behind.

As ever, the drive back home on the Sunday takes it out of me, but as soon as we get in, I'm back checking my calendar, looking to book days off work at a job I haven't even technically started yet. It's not much fun coming to terms with, but there might not be many opportunities left.

3

Bournemouth FC (Poppies) vs Blackfield & Langley

10 October 2020

THE WEEKEND in Bournemouth had been planned to perfection, but within hours of my money being wired to Trainline, those very plans were left in tatters, scattered like a Sammarinese defender up against world-class opposition. I suppose one of the biggest losses of the end of student life is the sudden end to the ability to go, 'Fuck it, I'm not going to come in today.' I don't think HSBC, where I've just started work, would be quite so accepting of this attitude. However, if you can finish work in London at 7pm and make it into a pub in Bournemouth within a couple of hours, it's not such a big deal. Unless, of course, the government decides within a day of you booking your tickets that all pubs have to shut at 10pm. Naturally, the plan is to go down anyway and hope the weather isn't quite as disastrous as it has been for all the rest of the days I've spent on the south coast that I can remember.

The show must go on.

At least I won't be on my own. I'm joined by Dan, a mate from Sutton United, university, Sunday league and basically everything else. Once down there, we're meeting Tom, another mate from uni. Despite being a reasonably good-looking guy (by our standards anyway), Tom raised eyebrows in our second year of university when he found a particularly attractive girlfriend. Flat-mates in first year, they got together at my 20th birthday party, a feat made particularly impressive by the fact Tom left that night after throwing up all over the garden of my new student house. The dynamic was made even more interesting for everyone by the fact I kept getting with her best friend every time we went out drinking as a group, despite the fact everyone reckoned she hated me when we were both sober. It's an assessment I can't exactly disagree with, either.

Tom and his girlfriend dated happily for a year and a half, and with Valentine's weekend coming up, she wanted a romantic weekend in Paris to celebrate. Unfortunately, this also happened to be the weekend a large group, including Dan and I, were heading up to Yorkshire to watch FC Halifax Town vs Sutton United. In a move that shocked and impressed everyone in equal measure, Tom dumped his stunning girlfriend in order to make the trip to watch some shit football with us. On the day, we made it as far as Sheffield before finding out the game had been postponed due to a waterlogged pitch.

If it wasn't for this pandemic, we'd be flat-mates up in central London by now. Instead, we're living at home, each of us feeling a little bit like life is passing us by. This weekend at least, things should feel a little bit like the old normal again. The train journey down to the south coast is anything but, though; eerily quiet to the point where we can blare music out loud without disturbing anyone. There's nobody in our carriage at all. The standard Friday night lager-drinking, makeup-perfecting, excitedly shouting revellers are nowhere to be seen; a sight of what feels like a bygone era. Dan and I sip on our cans of Heineken, feeling like two blokes expecting to find a huge party but turning up to the wrong house.

If truth be told, I planned this trip initially to watch Sutton down at Weymouth in what would have been the third game of the season, and the first proper away trip. The trouble was, there was no confirmation that Sutton's season was going to start at all. When I booked the trip, fans were still only allowed in at games at or below the seventh tier. The FA Vase is safe, of course, but the National League is classed as 'elite football', and after a slight uptick in cases, the government became hesitant on the October deadline for allowing fans back in. Whoever applied this 'elite' status clearly hadn't watched either of our 0-0 draws with Stockport County last season, that's all I'm saying. Typically, this element of the trip turned south pretty soon as well, and less than a week before we were due to return to action we were told fans could not attend. A government rescue package was agreed to allow the team to start the season, but supporters were only able to watch via a live stream.

Quite frankly, fuck that.

The plan had been to keep up on my FA Vase commitments with a Sunday fixture immediately after my Sunday league game, but the whole weekend has opened up now. Bournemouth FC vs Blackfield & Langley it is.

The phrase 'life is what you make it' annoys me, yet I can't help admit it's got a newfound relevance now. By the time our train eventually arrives in Bournemouth and we catch up with Tom, it's already gone 10pm; the town centre now a ghost town. It feels like the early hours of the morning, as if we should be heading straight off to bed already, but there are no plans for an early night just yet. After all, this is the first time I've managed to catch up with Tom since the height of lockdown. Duly graduating with the grades required, he was all set for a recruitment job in the city in July. With myself and Dan also finding jobs in the same area, the stage was set for a *Peep Show*-esque continuation of life after university and an escape from the monotony of living at home in a village with one pub and a postbox as its highlights. The only trouble is, Tom needs to be in his office to start his role. In July, we were told he was set for a September start, but as with everything else Covid-related, people have all the knowledge of Joey Essex in a Latin class. Now in mid-October, nobody is none the wiser as to when Tom can actually start.

Still, though, I really can't complain. While I've been able to start my job online, Tom has been balancing no fewer than four different jobs to earn some money. One day he's a delivery driver, the next a conservatory blogger, the next doing odd jobs for some OAPs who can't leave the house to do them themselves. As he guides us seamlessly to our hotel and on through the shortcut to the beach, I can't help but think he should try the tourist board for his next temporary role.

Bournemouth beach is beautiful by night. The moonlight glistens on the waves, with the bright lights of several stranded cruise ships marking out the horizon. The vast stretches of sand look serene with nobody there to ruin them but us. The only sound is the gentle lapping of the waves on the shore, and for a while the three of us just sit there in silence and take it in. It can't last, though – I've brought a football down to Bournemouth with me. Somehow, in my head anyway, a kickabout with mates is more peaceful than the sound of the ocean. I doubt they'd make a therapeutic sleep CD of me slicing a pass wide of Dan and laughing as he scampers after it, though. There's a romantic side to it, something that takes you back to days of your life before you had to worry about working four jobs, or indeed any jobs at all. Finishing a day at school and heading straight to the estate where your mates live, playing football using a lamp-post with a 'No Ball Games' sign as one of the two goalposts. Simple times.

Football at my primary school was something taken very seriously indeed. Each of the kids – boys and girls – split into their own teams that resembled a younger and slightly more benign version of street gangs. Whether five-a-side or 15-a-side, games were played at every morning and lunch break, and were always fiercely competitive. It got to the point where they had to call a whole school meeting to tell the Vultures and the Falcons not to play each other any more due to the large brawl that had broken out in the last fixture. No wonder, I thought, given we'd battered them about 24-0. The Falcons never did take defeat well. To this day, the sight of a falcon on TV makes me boil with rage.

All of this football rubbed off on our school team, though, and we were extremely successful. With me as captain, we defied all the odds to reach the final of Surrey

Schools, cruising past several of the favourites on the way. The final was an occasion to savour – we walked out to the Champions League theme tune from the tents that were acting as changing rooms, with a reasonably sized crowd and even a local newspaper reporter watching on. Sadly, that was as good as it got. We lost 2-1 to two goalkeeping errors, and I cried for the rest of the week. To make things worse, we never got any recognition in school assembly as the girls' team had also reached the Surrey Schools final, but had won it. I couldn't watch as they walked up on stage to show off their trophies when all I had to offer was a crappy runners-up medal. In fact, I didn't even have that to offer any more, having thrown it out as soon as I'd got home. Several of my team-mates were picked up by academies, while I spent the rest of my youth football days with Claygate Royals.

At least after childhood kickabouts, you didn't wake up in the morning with a raging hangover ahead of another full day's drinking. Last night's fun and games swung from wall-ball to a game of hitting an empty beer can from 50 yards away, as night gradually turned into day. The 10am checkout time means we're turfed out on to the streets with only a couple of hours' sleep, drifting around like lost travellers in search of an oasis. Eventually, and again with Tom's guidance, we find that oasis in the form of the Parkstone and Heatherlands, the Wetherspoons pub on Winton High Street, not far from where Bournemouth FC play.

Talk of football in the town of Bournemouth probably conjures up ideas of AFC Bournemouth, who of course famously climbed from the depths of League Two to reach the Premier League under Eddie Howe. Staying there for five seasons before relegation to the Championship, the club captured the hearts of the nation with their classic underdog story, even though they had benefitted from the investment of Maxim Demin. For all their recent glory, AFC Bournemouth are actually 24 years the junior of the two sides in the town. Bournemouth FC played their first fixture in 1875, while their now more successful neighbours were still just a glint in the eye of their first president Mr J.C. Nutt. The fates of the two different clubs hit 'sliding doors' point just after the conclusion of the First World War. AFC Bournemouth (then known as Boscombe) won the Hampshire League in 1920 and took promotion to the Southern League. Bournemouth FC then won it the following year, but did not take promotion. Three years later, Boscombe had been elected to the newly expanded Third Division South in the Football League, and the rest is history.

Speaking to Tom, and an elderly gentleman in the pub who invites himself into our conversation, it's clear where Bournemouth FC are in terms of stature now. Nobody seems to care. Most people in the town have probably never even heard of them. The success of their more illustrious near-neighbours has airbrushed them out of the picture. Give them a trip to Wembley in the FA Vase, though, and everything could change.

The elderly gentleman introduces himself as Morris, or 'Mau-REES if you're posh'. We're most certainly not, so Morris it is. With HATE tattooed across the knuckles of his left fist, marching around the pub as if he owns the place, he certainly seems a character. His thick farmer's accent betrays the fact he is a born and bred local, as does the flat cap, which he uses to cover his tipple when he goes on the long journey to the toilet. Obviously knowing the service is not the quickest, as we soon find out ourselves, he orders three pints of ale at a time and knocks them back with remarkable speed.

'Fuck it, I've had a good innings anyway. I'm 85, you know. Back when I was your age, you could get a pint for six shillings, none of this four-pounds-a-pint bollocks, and what's more…'

This goes on for quite some time. Some of the stories he tells are interesting, some bizarre, and others clearly bullshit. I don't mind it, though. This pandemic is a lonely time for anyone, and with constant shielding the mantra for the elderly, it must be particularly bad for them. I don't envy my grandad. I hope for his sake at least the pubs don't shut again. Morris drifts off into tales of going out drinking with members of Southampton's FA Cup-winning side of 1976 as the drinks continue to flow to our table. Tales of the wartime experiences of a young child follow as the clock ticks towards 2pm. Bournemouth FC have rather ambitiously told any supporters planning to attend today's game to arrive early, but Tom is unconcerned. Staying very much put in the pub, we spot the humorously typical non-league sight of several Blackfield & Langley players disappearing into the bookies across the road from the pub with barely an hour until kick-off.

To the outside observer, today's visitors might appear one of the favourites for the whole competition. The Watersiders had been playing two divisions up from the FA Vase requirement in the 2019/20 season, but had taken a voluntary relegation at the end of it to drop back down to the Wessex League and the ninth tier of English football. Vice-chairman Hans McDonald argued in June that the move was due to the high cost of travel and ground improvements at that level, but this would be rather overlooking the significance of losing their main investor Sam Davies, as well as the manager and several of the first-team squad, to rivals AFC Totton. Having shot up through the levels with two straight promotions to a position above what you might call their natural level, clearly McDonald feared a season of hammerings and wanted to put his side on a more level playing field. Though they've started the season at this new lower level reasonably well, the squad upheaval over the summer means this outsider favourites tag might be a bit wide of the mark. But this is cup football. You never know.

There's time for one more pub before the game starts, the Lark Rise, the highlight of which is some joker putting on 'Don't Stand So Close to Me' by the Police on the jukebox. I crack a smile, but it's a wry smile. Inside, I don't know whether to laugh or cry. Neither do most of the other drinkers, doing their best to ignore it and staring straight down into their pints, the only sign they've noticed it at all being a few under-the-breath mutters along the lines of 'fackin' hell'.

Walking down to the ground, it's clear Winton is a big student area. The giveaways are the empty cans of lager strewn across the pavements, the overgrown front gardens in large-but-tatty houses, and the general aura of the whole area having a hangover. Ahead of us are a group of about 20 lads of university age heading to the game as well, but my first thought is they might be a group of AFC Bournemouth fans looking for something to do on the international break weekend. Students don't really bother with football. In all my years at university, Tom and Dan were the only other match-going fans I met, and you don't half meet a lot of people at uni. Middle-class suburbia doesn't mix with working-class grit, or so it seems.

We catch up with them on the way in, and I'm wrong. If truth be told, I can tell the answer to my question on the first word the representative from the group says, as he speaks in a thick Brummie accent. A local he is not. The student explains that the group of friends came down to their first game on Wednesday night, and that the Bournemouth players loved having somebody there to support them. In just three days, they've become the self-styled 'Poppies Ultras' and have pledged their support to their student accommodation's local club. As the teams run out for kick-off, his bold words seem to be vindicated as the home players come over to acknowledge the group, the captain thanking them for coming down. It's smiles all round: I don't know how much football these guys usually watch, but it could easily be only the second time some have been to a game at all, and certainly one of the first times they've felt a real part of it.

In many ways, non-league football is in danger of becoming slightly trendy. The previous week has seen the Premier League decide to charge £14.95 per game for a streaming service of games not shown on TV. Understandably, this has led to outrage at the greed of it all, but it wouldn't be the first time. For many people, I suppose it's a game of greed Buckaroo. How much can the Premier League take the piss out of you before you get sick of it and go somewhere you're appreciated? Somewhere you can get a match ticket, pie and pint for less than the £15 it costs to watch West Brom vs Burnley on a dodgy stream. Somewhere you can meet up with mates, and then drink with the players after the game. Somewhere you can walk home from when you've had a few in the bar. Crowds are starting to rise in the lower leagues as loyal fans get pushed over this bullshit threshold, and I'm sure this trend will continue as the cash-rich clubs at the top seek out even more of their share of the pie. At any rate, students getting involved is definitely a harbinger of the trendy apocalypse.

Sadly, the rest of the town doesn't seem to have got the memo. Lump me, Tom and Dan in with the students and we make up about half the crowd. The rest mostly comprises old blokes, dotted around and showing a more passive interest in the game than the Poppies Ultras do. I can see why Blackfield & Langley wanted to drop down the divisions too – as far as I can tell, not a single away fan has made the 30-mile trip from the Solent today.

I've heard football grounds described as 'homely' before, but for many people they could describe Victoria Park in this way and be talking quite literally. On three sides of the ground there are houses backing on to the grassed spectator area, and each and every back garden has a gate into the stadium. It's the supporter's dream. You could spill out of bed after a heavy night out at 2.58pm and still be inside the ground for kick-off. Rainy day? Simply watch the game from your upstairs bedroom window instead. When Bill Shankly talked about Everton playing at the bottom of his garden, I wonder if this is what he was envisaging.

Originally a farmer's field, Victoria Park has been home to Bournemouth FC since 1890, and it would appear not much has changed since then. There is just the one designated structure for spectators, a seated main stand constructed after the original burnt down in 1974. Otherwise, the only difference to a Sunday morning venue is the metal barrier separating the pitch from the viewing area. Cars park at the back of the expansive grass area behind one goal, though not far away enough from the pitch that they're safe from wayward shots. The area up the other side is used by some kids for an impromptu kickabout space as the main game is about to start. Hardly keeping a watchful eye, the parents sit in the glass-walled bar next to the main stand, which affords a view of the game as good as any from outside against the railings.

Despite the beauty of the setup, there are no faces in windows watching the game. The only sign of life in these houses at all is the low buzz of a lawnmower coming from a garden as the ref blows his whistle to start the match. The gates remain firmly closed. The locals have drawn the curtains. The match itself offers justification for this approach in the early stages. The ball moves like a rugby ball on an uneven pitch, tackles thunder in, and much effort is exerted without anything of note actually happening. One of the visiting team's substitutes jogs up the touchline purely to have a go at the students behind the goal.

'Imagine wasting your time coming to watch Poppies.'

'Fuck off, you midget. At least we can drink.'

When Tom points out that in being a substitute, the Blackfield & Langley player is just as guilty of wasting time watching the Poppies as anyone else there, he turns his attention to us instead. I have awful visions of this guy coming off the bench to nick a winner at Wembley and find already my neutral position has most definitely shifted. The back-and-forth goes on, becoming more and more tedious, until finally something happens on the pitch to break it up.

Blackfield are on the attack and looking dangerous when suddenly the referee's whistle blows. It takes everyone a second to work out what's going on, but it all becomes clear when everyone on the pitch runs towards where two players are on the floor, grappling and landing punches on each other. The substitutes also disappear to enter the fray, and it takes a minute to clear. The result is a red card apiece; both sides down to ten men for the rest of the game. In fairness, I've often seen red cards for just a gentle raise of the hand to someone's face, so if you are going to get sent off you might as well do it properly, I suppose. Both teams still having the same numbers on the pitch keeps it fair too, and it might even open the game up a bit. God knows it needs it. As the two dismissed players disappear out of sight, everyone on the pitch rushes over again. From where we are, there's nothing to see with the tunnel obscuring the action, but the shouting gives it away as the two sets of players pile into each other again.

'I think he'll have to abandon the game, it's a bloody disgrace,' says the bloke next to us to nobody in particular. 'Why the ref sent them both down the tunnel at the same time, I'll never know.'

It's exactly the sort of incident a football commentator would describe as 'not what you want to see' when everyone sat at home is thinking that it's exactly the sort of thing they want to see. So long as he doesn't abandon the game, that is.

Eventually, everyone emerges again. At least I think it's everyone. Within seconds of the game starting again, Blackfield & Langley take the lead. I've got to be honest: I didn't really see what happened, as I was still trying to count how many players on each side had actually re-emerged from the tunnel. Apparently, the Poppies' keeper had managed to boot the ball against his own defender, allowing the quirkily named River Smith to pick up the loose ball and tap in. It sounds exactly the sort of goal befitting the match. As I finish counting the players, it is confirmed that nine-man Blackfield & Langley have the lead against ten-man Bournemouth FC.

'They've lost their heads' is one of the oldest clichés in the footballing book, but Bournemouth really epitomise it today as they go 2-0 down just a minute later. This time, I see all there is to see, and it's shocking. Ali Zintany is allowed the freedom of the town to run into the box, stop for a cup of tea and a biscuit, and then slot into the bottom corner. The referee probably does the Poppies a favour when he blows for half-time several minutes early, presumably to stop the game descending further into farce. The mouthy substitute on the touchline is loving it, making sure he jogs up to the students gathered behind the goal before heading the other way to join the rest of his team. Unfortunately for him, in the heat of the moment, he leaves his tracksuit top by the side of the pitch as he disappears off down the tunnel. I can't imagine it will still be there when he returns.

Frustratingly, the home side do nothing to shut the new pantomime villain up in the early exchanges of the second half. Passes go astray; shots end up in back gardens; Blackfield look untroubled. There are still no faces at windows, and even the students behind the goal fall into something of a lull. Only the seemingly random shouts of 'YOU'RE IN' from the visitors' dugout punctuate the silence. The worst one is called with the ball still inside Blackfield & Langley's own half. I feel like it has to be that substitute taking the piss; nobody is that stupid in reality. Just as the game seems to be over, an innocuous Bournemouth free kick from more or less the halfway line is floated into the box and flicked past the stranded keeper into the net. With ten minutes to go, the whole place bursts into life. Players and supporters bounce off each other, the noise rising, the pressure building in turn. The midfield start to win challenges they've been second to all game, passes have extra conviction, the coaching team are animated. The words from the Blackfield & Langley dugout and indeed players have changed too.

'Ref. REF. How fucking long, ref?'

Five minutes. Enough. As the pressure builds, tricky Poppies winger Jonathan Efedje moves inside the box. Just as he goes to pull the trigger, he collapses to the ground. All eyes turn to the referee.

Penalty.

The wait to take it as the defender pleads his innocence ramps up the sense of anticipation even more. I actually feel slightly nervous for them myself, not least because of the actions of my mates. Tom has taken a gamble, running over to the Blackfield & Langley bench already to give it large to that substitute. Miss now, and he's going to look a right idiot. Lewis Harvey, a defender, is the man to step up and take the pressure for his side. He scuffs the ball, but somehow it squirms underneath the keeper and just about across the line. The students go mad; Tom presumably goes mad, though I've stayed well out of the way of the whole thing. Eventually, the jubilant players grab the ball and bring it back to the centre circle to have one last go at their nine-man opposition. As the game kicks off again, I get a notification from my phone – 'GOAL: Weymouth 0-1 Sutton United'. It must appear to the rest of the crowd as if I have severely delayed reactions, jumping around and punching the air a minute after the Bournemouth goal has gone in. To be honest, I couldn't care less what it looks like. I'd love to be there, don't get me wrong, but it makes it that little bit easier if we're winning the games.

The added time in the Bournemouth game is generous, but nowhere near as much as slightly further down the south coast in Weymouth. Rather than Bournemouth, there's time for the visitors to nearly sneak a winner, but player-manager Fawzi Saadi can only curl his shot wide on the break. As the game goes to penalties, six minutes are added on down in Weymouth. Fortunately for him, Tom is not caught up in the ins and outs of another game several miles away. He mooches back around to where we're standing with a smug grin on his face as the full-time whistle goes. As we head towards the goal where the spot-kicks are due to be taken, the story of what happened at the dugout comes out. In short, the mouthy substitute didn't take it in good heart. This pleases me, but there's pressure on the shoot-out now all right. Another thing to worry about. All I can do is resign myself to the fact I'm powerless over both outcomes and sit back to either enjoy or endure whatever fate might greet me.

One group who haven't resigned themselves, though, are the students. Quite the opposite, in fact. Lined up along the barrier behind the goal, they try nearly every trick in the book to put off the Blackfield & Langley takers. There's shouting, arm-waving, sharp little digs, the lot. All that's left is for someone to get their arse out, but thankfully we don't get that far. Finally, faces appear at the window of one of the houses behind the goal, more students by the look of it. Though late to this party, it seems they might be off to another one tonight as they neck a can of lager each while one lad spends nearly the whole shoot-out doing his hair. Even the kids enjoying their kickabout behind the goal break it off to wander over and watch the action.

Bournemouth get off to the perfect start, Lewis Harvey with a more convincing penalty this time. The Blackfield player up next steps up to a volley of abuse, and his penalty is saved – advantage Bournemouth. It doesn't last, though, as the second Poppies penalty is saved.

'Go on, JJ,' comes the call from the line of the remaining Blackfield players on the halfway line as their next taker steps up.

'Fuck off, JJ,' call back at least three of the students, to cries of laughter from all those around them. JJ looks nervous; the keeper and indeed the students smell blood. He steps up, and skies the ball so far over the bar the students watching from the house behind the goal flinch. Even though the keeper hasn't had a part to play in this miss, you can feel the sense of victory from behind the goal. 'We did this, we made him miss.' Meanwhile, according to the LiveScore app, the Sutton game keeps going, the six minutes up but still no full-time whistle.

The next four penalties are tucked away, leaving Bournemouth with a chance to win it on their final spot-kick. Their main man from the 90 minutes, Jonathan Efedje, is the man to step up. It's written in the stars; it has to be. The excitement among the throng of student supporters behind the goal is palpable, already planning their celebrations. Meanwhile, the Blackfield & Langley bench shrink away, focusing more on planning a quick exit than any celebrations. The wait goes on and on, which only serves to bring the excitement behind the goal closer to frenzy point. Finally, Efedje steps up, and his weak effort is saved by the keeper.

Blackfield score their penalty, and we head to sudden death. I can't believe it, nobody can. That away team bench if they go on to win this now.

The Poppies score, putting the pressure back on, but the next taker in green and white has no issue with levelling up. The Sutton game is still fucking going. Screaming at the ref to blow up internally just isn't the same as being there. The Poppies score again. More in hope than expectation, the students target the next Blackfield taker; one slip-up from him and the tie is gone. Just as he starts his run-up, I get the notification – 'Full time: Weymouth 0-1 Sutton United'. My celebrations are apt for the scene seconds later in Bournemouth too, as the penalty is saved by the keeper.

Finally, the celebrations that have been so tantalisingly threatening since the equaliser went in get to fully erupt. It's a great sight as the fans spill on to the pitch, jumping around with the players, whooping and hollering and generally just enjoying themselves. It might be the FA Vase, but you can see in each of the players' heads they've just become top-level professionals for the day, living the hero role with their adulating followers praising them to the high heavens. With news of the Sutton win putting wind in my sails, I even jump the barrier on to the pitch myself, though leaving the group celebration to those already in the midst of it. By the time it dies down, Blackfield & Langley have disappeared. One courteous player remains to shake the hands of the jubilant home players, but he's very much alone. The mouthy substitute must feel like a right twat. The only disappointment of the game is that he doesn't stick about long enough for us to rub it in.

The train home isn't for another four hours, and as the beers keep flowing, the day just feels better and better. We lurch from pub to pub, talking football, football and more football. When it's finally time to say goodbye, we're like long-distance lovers, 'We'll meet again soon, stay in touch, love you!' The journey back with Dan is spent in an alcohol-fuelled stupor, as we float back towards London once more.

* * *

BEEPBEEPBEEPBEEP.

Another early alarm, another particularly unwelcome wake-up call. It's Sunday morning. That means Sunday league. It sounded a lot more fun signing up back in August, before you actually had to get out of bed with a shocking hangover to trudge over to some sodden playing field in the middle of nowhere and get trounced 6-0. In fact, the two games we've played so far this season have been even worse than that – we got beat by 11 goals on the opening day, and haven't scored a goal ourselves yet. The joys.

I remember bits of the train journey home. There was one bloke who asked to use my phone charger, as his iPhone had died sometime ago. As soon as he managed to get it live again, he received a call from an angry-sounding female voice, presumably his girlfriend. For some reason, the none-too-sober bloke decided to put the call on speaker, as if proud of the situation he was about to find himself in.

'It's your flat-mate's birthday, you were meant to be here at six, you wanker!'

'Heeeeyyyyyy, Johnnie, tell the nice lady we're nearly at Woking.'

We weren't nearly at Woking.

'Er, yeah, next stop, I think. I'm sure he'll be there soon.'

'We'll talk later, James.'

I didn't envy the guy as the phone was hung up on him. Sitting in bed in the morning, with a glass of water and feeling sorry for myself, it does help me feel a little better, though. As the call finished, I recall asking James if he wanted to plug his phone back in again. After a little theatrical hands-on-face thinking process, he turned round and told me he'd decided against it, thinking it was probably for the best if he just let it die again. There is always someone worse off than yourself, and I wouldn't swap places with James this morning even if Barcelona turned out as our opponents at Prince George's Playing Fields.

Luckily, it's not Barcelona we're facing, but Royal Oak from down the road in Tolworth. We lose again and I have to go off with a hamstring injury ten minutes in, but there is still a definite highlight of the morning: Dan turning up in a fetching new green and white Blackfield & Langley tracksuit top.

4

Coventry Sphinx vs Heanor Town

31 October 2020

THEY SAY that your university days are the best of your life, which even as arguably the world's biggest pessimist I find a bit much. 'It's all downhill from here, mate,' they say. 'The best days have been and gone and they aren't ever coming back.' I would be lying if I said I was completely spared these post-uni blues, especially as the coronavirus situation takes away the buffer completely. There's no soft landing any more, no bar crawls in upmarket London, or any clubbing last hurrahs before you become old enough to be classed as weird in a club full of teenagers. At the minute, there's nothing at all. Wake up, do a day's work from your bedroom, eat dinner, watch the telly and go to bed, all on an indefinite loop. You can see why mental health problems among young people are going through the roof.

Admittedly, a fair chunk of my particular university experience was some way away from being the best days of my life; in fact, I'd like to keep it as the worst for as long as possible. I certainly can't blame my mates for that one, though, and I've got three of them travelling up to the West Midlands with me this weekend. Dan, now hooked by the FA Vase journey, is one of them, and he's joined by two of my former flat-mates, Louis and Adil. Both are now in the job search, in a market as unforgiving as a North Korean dictator. While I work a paid 9-5 role, they both regularly spend the same amount of time in a day simply looking for a job that will pay them anything at all. I certainly don't envy them. Though we were in Coventry for the years we lived together, the plan is to stay in the other main student town, Leamington Spa, this weekend. Quite simply, Coventry is not a happy place for me.

Unfortunately, arriving into town at 9pm doesn't get you very far these days, with the curfew just an hour later still in place. There's countless people I've not seen in months who I want to catch up with, but no real time in which to do it. Barely 24 hours later, I'll be on a train back down to London, where I will be back on my own once more, the break from reality very much a brief excursion. For once, though, the rules are on our side – Leamington is still a tier one area and we can meet outside, or even indoors, if we keep to no more than six people in each of our hotel rooms. It starts to become tactical – who will come if they are asked along? Will they bring anyone? Will we actually get caught if we do go over the magic number of 12? I don't fancy one of those £10,000 fines that have been handed out to students guilty of breaking the rules. Eventually, the invites are sent out via Facebook Messenger as last orders are called, and we can sit back and wait for the night to fall into place.

Waiting isn't any fun, though, and our group of four friends messing about is as inevitable as the setting of the sun at the end of the day. Somehow, Dan is convinced that a prank call to the Babestation channel available on the hotel TV is a good idea, the ultimate mission to ask who would win in a fight between a German Shepherd and a bald eagle. Sheephead from *Soccer AM* is the inspiration, in particular his call to Babeworld to talk about Viennese whirls. If you're not familiar with the video, it's well worth a look, I promise you that. Unfortunately, we're not experts on prank calls to adult TV in quite the same way Sheephead is. It might look smooth in that master version, but the reality of getting Dan to give it a go himself is quite far removed from that success. Getting connected to the line is virtually impossible, a series of options and credit card details as the girl sits on screen with not a single call coming through. After 20 minutes, she actually gets replaced by another model, which seems harsh given we've been trying to connect the whole time. When we eventually get on to the line, all this new model does in response to the question is groan and take her minimal remaining clothes off. The golden question remains sadly unanswered.

Dan gives up, and we sit there feeling a bit underwhelmed. Seconds later, he receives a text and cries out in horror.

'They've charged me £47 for that! It only said £2 a minute! Oh Jesus, my dad is still the bill payer as well. How am I going to explain this to him? What shall I do?'

In all honesty, this episode is far funnier than the original call itself. Bravely, Dan opts to deny knowledge of the transaction and goes through to a call with his bank. The rest of us sit there in silence, our concentration captured by the sheer hilarity of what is now going on. Seemingly unbothered by our complete lack of sympathy, Dan puts the call on speakerphone.

'Hi, this is Natalie from Barclays, can you confirm if you recognise the transaction recorded, please?'

'Erm, well, you see, me and my friends were sort of … well, we decided we would call Babestation AS A PRANK…'

I don't hear anything else of what's said, as I'm too busy rolling around on the floor in stitches. A few minutes later, we get the text saying the first of our guests is at the downstairs door of our hotel, and the night moves swiftly on. Before we know it, it's 3.30am and the sizeable bins in each of our two rooms are both full to the brim with cans and bottles of just about any type of alcohol imaginable. It's fair to say the next morning hits hard, but it's undoubtedly worth it for the much-needed release that it delivers in style.

The footballing plan for the weekend had been to visit Racing Club Warwick, for their fixture at home to Stoke-based Abbey Hulton United. However, their tie was soon switched to Abbey Hulton for some reason, leaving us with little choice but to head to Coventry Sphinx vs Heanor Town. It means I've got to go to the Coventry University side of town for the first time since second year.

My first year of university, in the most horrifically clichéd way possible, was about finding myself. Living away from home for the first time and free from the strange environment of an all-boys school, the possibilities were pretty much limitless. In a way, though, it became the life equivalent of trying to down 15 shots of sambuca all at the same time. With anything possible, missing out on something made me a failure in my own head. I wanted to socialise with my flat-mates, my course-mates, my football team, watch Sutton United back at home with my mates, play sport, join societies and try and get a decent degree on top of all this. The result, more often than not, was breakdown, the stress bringing the tears up to the surface time after time. Not once did I ever think to get help. I simply didn't have the time.

The summer holidays gave me a chance to breathe once the year was over, creating a chance to reassess what I was doing. Things obviously weren't right, that was clear for anybody to see, but in my head I had the perfect solution. Aged 19, I still hadn't ever been in a proper committed relationship in my whole life. A girlfriend would sort me out, anchoring me to something meaningful and stopping me chasing shadows my entire life. I now had a new, more gaping, missing piece to fill.

Three months into second year and still desperately single, somehow everything and yet still ultimately nothing had changed. From assessing myself on an impossible quota of tasks, the only metric for success now was finding love, and I was failing at both. One thought would grow into another, expanding and intensifying in an iron grip around my brain.

Nobody would ever want to be with you. What kind of loser can't find a girlfriend at university anyway? You're going to be alone for ever.

On Tuesday, 4 December 2018, still lost in the labyrinth of my mind, I decided to venture off to the Midland Football League's main local derby: Coventry Sphinx vs Coventry United. Though an entertaining game, it was impossible to enjoy with the thoughts racing around my head making me feel like an outcast, an oddball. Normal students don't go to ninth-tier football matches on their own; they're out partying, drinking, having a good time. Trudging back to our dark and desolate house, past the bright lights and laughter of the new student flats in the city centre, I wanted nothing more than to swap places with one of these happy-go-lucky freshers and start all over again. The next evening, on a more conventional student trip to a city centre nightclub to make myself feel normal again more than anything else, things finally took a turn.

Back in the hotel in Leamington, nursing a hangover with a large full English breakfast, I know how weird it will feel to be back at Sphinx Drive in vaguely familiar territory. As it happens, so do my companions for the day, and the piss-taking forces me back to life as we stagger down the street and on to the station platform to jump on a train to memory lane. The train station in Coventry is right in the middle of a city dominated by students, and once exiting on to the concourse you have a choice. Turn left to go west, and you head towards the suburb dominated by students at the University of Warwick: Earlsdon, where I lived. Turn right, or pretty much anywhere else, and you end up in Coventry University territory. Coventry Sphinx's modest home ground is deep into the latter of the two areas. The worlds of the two universities in general rarely collide but could not have been closer for me in that second year.

Georgina, it seemed, was absolutely perfect for me. A big fan of her sport, and football in particular, it was fitting that we'd met on indie night at the Empire, as we also shared an almost identical taste in music. The first few dates we went on were almost impossibly successful, as we could talk all night on these shared interests we had. We shared our first kiss under the moonlight outside her house, and this time I walked home in a different kind of daze. Everything would be all right; it would all fall into place. She was a Coventry student, me a Warwick student, creating a type of university *Romeo and Juliet* situation for which we got stick, but neither of us cared one bit. Twice a week, we would hit the bars on Far Gosford Street in the centre of Coventry, throwing pound after pound into the jukebox and holding our own shocking two-person karaoke in the corner. On our third date, after a surprisingly strong rendition of James Blunt's 'Stay the Night', my reward was exactly that.

The weather as we pull into Coventry station is fitting for the mood as the skies open, dark clouds giving way to torrential rain that makes the five-minute walk to the pub seem like an age. Far Gosford Street has changed since the winter of 2018, with new buildings springing up on every street corner. The Coventry University buildings still dominate, though; ugly and overbearing in what might otherwise be a reasonably nice place. The pubs we plan to visit ahead of the game are the exact same ones I went to with Georgina. After nearly two years, it's time to face things head-on rather than avoid the best pubs because of the memories that come with them. In fact, I've planned a drinking route that visits all four of the pubs she introduced me to.

Most people would have realised after just a few weeks of dating that things weren't quite right, but then I wasn't quite right, either. This was my missing piece. I was a man now, a proper man. All I needed to turn my life around was to find a girlfriend, and I had done it. That was it. The world was perfect, I would be happy until the day I died, and any countering thoughts I would quash as I did with any sense of hope I'd desperately searched for before we met. A month in and we were still together but talking a lot less. We grew distant, which terrified me, and I hoped and prayed for something to change. It didn't. Two days before Valentine's Day, Georgina made a rare trip round to my house, rather than me having to trek over to visit her. She told me that she'd realised she just wasn't that attracted to me. She said she was sorry, we hugged, and she left.

Nobody could understand quite why I was so down in the weeks and months that followed. After all, we'd only been together a few months. Plenty more fish in the sea and all that. But for me it was too late, my mind already cast back to thinking of that Coventry Sphinx game back in December 2018, but even worse. As the Arctic Monkeys once sang, 'The knife twists at the thought that I should fall short of the mark.' Not only was I alone again, but I also wasn't good enough. Not good enough as a lover, not good enough as a man. This time, it really felt like there was no way out.

Looking back, now I too can see my thinking was all over the place, and that really I wasn't well. They say time is a healer, though the counselling I had certainly helped too, and these days I feel a lot better. One thing I never did do, though, was go back to the pubs we visited together, and today feels like the final step on a psychological journey. The football itself is secondary.

The perfect outcome for the day is the group of us getting drunk and acting like idiots as normal, and it's clear from the off that's exactly what's going to happen. Before we even hit midday, Adil drops his double vodka and Coke on to the concrete floor of an otherwise empty pub, apologising profusely to the sole member of staff there as the rest of us offer no sympathy whatsoever. An hour later in the Wetherspoons, he orders a cranberry juice, but sits there silently after receiving a rum and Coke instead. It turns out this drink is meant for Dan, but he assumes it just hasn't arrived and goes up to the bar to complain, none the wiser that his drink is sat right next to him with Adil. He comes back triumphant with a new drink in hand just as Adil's cranberry juice finally arrives, and there's a moment of realisation as the pair clock just how stupid they've been. Still, Dan gets a free drink out of it, so there's no complaints from him.

Any wistful memories from the pubs we visit are overwritten by new happy, drunken ones as the day progresses. The Golden Cross, where Georgina and I went on our first date, becomes the pub where we lock Adil in a four-sided roll cage and push him round the smoking area until the landlord comes out and shouts at us. Quids Inn, the site of the James Blunt karaoke sessions, sees a shock victory for myself in a pool competition as music by the Enemy blares out in the background. There are plenty of happy couples dotted around each pub, but the sight of them doesn't bother me as it might have done a year ago. When we finally collapse into the taxi to the ground with a quarter of an hour to go until kick-off, spirits are high. Whatever happens next, the day has been a success.

As we arrive at the ground the rain has eased off, which is a relief, as there's next to no cover there at all. The first-team pitch is one of many 11-a-side pitches on a muddy grass field, but is differentiated from the others by a small brick main stand on one side and a railing separating the pitch from the spectator area. On the far side, there's not even a concrete path to walk on, and our trainers are soon all coated in mud as we trudge round to get a good view of the game. Sadly, there is no time to have a pint in the impressive Sphinx Sports and Social Club that stands adjacent to the ground, a cavernous building with several rooms, all of them virtually empty today.

The home side are definitely the favourites today, despite facing a Heanor Town side exempt from the qualifying rounds on the back of last season's relatively strong performance in the competition. Sphinx play in the division above their opponents, who sit mid-table in the East Midlands Counties League.

The previous weekend saw a shock victory for the Coventry side, 2-1 away at title favourites Newark, and today's match programme wastes no time in bringing that up – though not in the way you might expect, 'After the match the sour reaction of various Newark fans and match reporters was cock-eyed and completely stupid. Sphinx's players, management, and supporters had quite rightly enjoyed the victory, condemned by the joyless hosts as over-celebrating. The next day we were reading about Sphinx winning their "cup final", not only a laughable misunderstanding of the situation but an indication to future opponents that Newark can be got at. They win often but they lose in a huff. The whole affair was quite pathetic and it's that mindset, that bitterness, that entitlement, that reveal when a club has ideas above its station. If you can't take defeat with dignity the Midland Football League Premier Division is going to be a punishing place for you.'

It's different to the usual 'welcome and enjoy the game' message, that's for sure. There's also a slight dig at city rivals Coventry United, who on Tuesday night recorded 'their first win over Sphinx for some time'. United are the upstarts of non-league football in Coventry, founded by Coventry City fans disgruntled at the club's move away from the Ricoh Arena in 2013. Three consecutive promotions brought the club into the Midland Football League Premier Division, disrupting Sphinx's dominance of Coventry's non-league scene. The two clubs are now bitter rivals, with the blue and white of Coventry Sphinx starting to slip behind in the local hierarchy. This can be highlighted by looking at the crowds at Sphinx's last two home games. A league fixture against Selston attracted just 65 spectators, whereas Tuesday's fixture against Coventry United saw a Covid-compliant sell-out of 300. My student house was only a couple of minutes away from Butts Park Arena, the Earlsdon home of Coventry United, and so I've very much taken sides already – I'm behind Heanor today. The others, less into their local football than me, opt to back the home side.

The underdogs start brightly and nearly take the lead inside the opening minute, but the ball is eventually scrambled to safety by a relieved home defender. Sadly, this is as good as it gets for Heanor and within five minutes, they're already 2-0 down. The goals come so early that I miss the first one, still walking round to the other side of the ground, and only catch the tail end of the second one as the ball rolls slowly across the line. According to the old bloke standing next to me when we do eventually pick a spot, the first goal was a screamer, but the second was a shocking error from the visitors' debutant keeper, who cleared the ball straight into the arse of the Coventry forward and was left only able to watch on in horror as the ball crossed the line. Any hopes of the game being an entertaining contest are virtually over already.

Not that this bothers my mates, though. 'This is much better than sitting and watching TV,' muses Adil, who normally has no interest in watching football whatsoever. As we chat casually among ourselves, a sense of normality is created in a world that is anything but. Ironically, it was normality that I so dearly craved last time I attended a fixture here, but not quite like this.

The sky blue and white stripes of Coventry Sphinx swarm all over their opponents, threatening further scoring. The poor Heanor keeper's debut day gets even worse as he fumbles a corner after 25 minutes, and the ball ends up in the back of the net for 3-0. Two minutes later, another corner results in another scramble, which results in another goal. It really is shocking stuff as far as the visitors are concerned, but Coventry won't mind one bit as they look set to cruise through to the next round. Despite this dominance, there are no delusions of grandeur from the home supporters and staff. I ask one guy, tasked with telling us to stop sipping our cans of Carling in view of the pitch as FA rules forbid it apparently, how he rates his side's chances of making it through to a Wembley final. 'Slim' is his response. 'It's always one of those bloody northern teams.'

As if responding to his cynicism, Sphinx make it 5-0, an incredible lob from inside his own half by Madundo Semahimbo sparking an otherwise indifferent crowd into cries of jubilation and rounded applause. We're still barely half an hour in.

With no end to the attacking onslaught in sight, the conversation among us turns to how bad we think the scoreline will get. I'm revising my pre-match prediction from 5-0 to 8-0, while Louis and Adil are both hopeful that their new adopted side can hit double figures by the end of the day. Take nothing away from Coventry Sphinx, but I can't help but secretly wish that this rare treat of a live football match was a bit closer. Maybe it's just the general dread of another lockdown getting to me, and I decide I'm going to make a conscious effort not to think about it while I am still out enjoying myself. Control the controllables. Use the coping strategies picked up in the aftermath of my second year at uni.

The spell of Sphinx domination is finally broken just before half-time, rendering all of the predictions we've just made completely irrelevant. A visiting centre-forward breaks through on goal, but he looks as surprised as anyone else in the ground and the moment of hesitation allows the covering full-back to get across. He's not quick enough, though, and clearly brings the Heanor man down just outside the area. It's the most blatant red card you'll ever see.

The referee doesn't seem to agree, though. He gives the foul but then trudges over to the linesman on the side we're standing on to discuss the incident. Coming under fire from the Sphinx faithful stood close to us, the two of them actually step forward on to the pitch to give themselves a bit of space. None of us can work out what it is they might be discussing; there really isn't anything to discuss. Finally, after a good couple of minutes of inane conversation, the referee walks back towards the players and shows the red card to Patsun Tufan, who doesn't even bother protesting as he heads off down the tunnel. As the remaining five minutes of the half peter out, I opt to pass the time by shouting at the linesman and asking what it is they were talking about during the red card delay. To my surprise, he actually turns round and answers my question as the ball is pumped up the other end of the pitch.

'We weren't fully sure if it was inside or outside the box, so we wanted to check with each other before making the decision.'

Bollocks, it was miles outside. I reckon they just fancied a quick chat. A chatty linesman is something of a lower-league novelty: most of the officials I've come across have had so much shouted at them that the only way to cover it all would be to turn round and stick two fingers up. Unsurprisingly, this is typically frowned upon, though not everyone takes this into account. Walking the dog a few years ago, I got talking to a former referee, a bloke in his 70s who used to do games at FA Vase level 20 years or so ago. I admitted I'd hate to do his job, with all the abuse from fans and players alike. 'It never bothered me,' he said, and without skipping a beat he added, 'I just told them all to fuck off.'

Mind you, officials in this country are the lucky ones. I went to a local derby between Spartak Trnava and Slovan Bratislava in Slovakia back in 2014. Slovan beat their fierce local rivals, with the linesman on the near side making a few calls that influenced the game, some controversial and some less so. Every time he made a call against Trnava, pints of lager were rained down on his head from the stand.

With away fans banned from attending, the police presence was all outside the ground, and nobody was interested in putting a stop to it. It's just as well it was a reasonably warm day, or the poor bloke might have ended up resembling one of the Heineken Extra Cold beer taps that always look so enticing in the pub after a match. I wonder if his wife had any strong questions for him when he got back, 'You said you were at work, but you stink of alcohol! What are you hiding from me, Jozef?'

When he told us to stop drinking our cans of Carling earlier, the enforcer graciously let us hold on to the booze on the condition we drink it outside the ground at half-time, so the second the whistle goes, we head off to do exactly that. The Sphinx Sports and Social Club looks the perfect place to do this – such is the size of the place, we find a room to sit in where we're literally the only ones in there. Presumably normally a function room, it looks frozen in time, prepared for an event that was never allowed to happen. Helium balloons droop and sag down from the ceiling, decorations still adorn the stage, but the shutters to the bar are firmly closed. It feels like an eerie sign of the times as we sit back and sip on our lagers once again.

After just a few minutes, the bloke who initially told us to drink outside the ground sticks his head round the door with the sort of look your parents give you when you crack open a beer at 10am on Christmas Day.

'You're gonna have to move, lads, it's three to a table. You shouldn't even be in here really.'

Unless the government has made an announcement since half-time, I don't know quite where he's picked this rule from, especially as we've all been standing together watching the game. We exchange quizzical looks but follow his instructions and move Louis and Adil to the table next to ours. The bloke isn't satisfied, though, and two minutes later he's back, this time with backup.

'Right, all of you, OUT. You can't drink your alcohol in here. You've been warned.'

Feeling a bit aggrieved, we find a spare ball and go for a kickabout while we wait for the second half to start. There are two full 11-a-side pitches right next to the first-team pitch, with nothing preventing you watching the game from here, and this allows a quick transition between knocking the ball about the side pitch during a break in play and moving back to keep an eye on the proper action. The can confiscator looks on with daggers in his eyes, intensifying when a stray pass from Adil nearly makes its way on to the pitch. By the time we give it up and go back to the pitchside railing to watch the game, we all feel a bit better.

Just as we start paying attention again, Heanor score, and their supporters that have taken over the stand on the near side celebrate as if they've just equalised rather than scored a probable consolation. It's a nice contrast to the relative nonchalance of the home support, but if it is a signal of optimism, I can't help but feel it's probably misplaced. Even with ten men, Coventry Sphinx are clearly a class above their opponents. They're a young side, with several players brought through from a successful academy, and play with a pace and intensity that Heanor struggle to match. The future of the club looks bright, that's for sure.

With a comeback ambitious at best, the game starts to lose its flow as it drifts towards its inevitable conclusion. Dan decides that each time there's a break in play he's going to drift off to the side pitch and have a go at hitting the crossbar. A substitution around the hour mark gives him his opportunity and, wasting no time, he jogs off with the ball to set himself up as the rest of us watch on, not expecting much. To our amazement, he thunders the ball off the bar from the halfway line with his first attempt, wheeling off in a celebration more extravagant than any following the goals in the main event. He even makes it back to our viewing point before the action gets under way again. I wonder if it might be worth Heanor taking a punt on him.

Despite the game being over as a contest, there's more drama, with the home side up in arms at what seemed an innocuous aerial challenge with not long left. The Sphinx player is left in pain, but it seemed to be an accidental collision rather than anything malicious, and if it wasn't for the actions of the home bench, I doubt the ref would even consider producing a yellow card. However, under constant bombardment from players, staff and fans alike, he goes for his default move of walking over to the linesman for a chat. With the baying mob demanding a red card, the ref gives in and duly obliges. The young Heanor player looks devastated, both at the red card and the fact he might have inadvertently seriously hurt the Coventry player, but is prevented from making a quick escape by the can confiscator from earlier. Throwing his cigarette to the ground in anger, he confronts the distraught young lad, spewing vile abuse until eventually somebody else does everyone a favour and pulls him away. Adil remarks, audibly but still only intended for our group, that this bloke is not the nicest of chaps.

'What the fuck are you here for anyway?' comes a loud shout from right next to us. 'Acting like dickheads, kicking the ball around during the game, fucking about, what's the point? Fucking students.'

The angry bald man spits at the ground and stares us down, his eyes bulging out of his beetroot face, as if daring us to say something back. I would love to say we had a witty response in reply, but that would be a bare-faced lie. None of us can believe quite how much he's just lost his head at something so small, and at 5-1 up as well. Dan mumbles something about seeing why Coventry United are so much bigger than Sphinx, and then we turn away and watch the next few minutes in silence. Deciding there are places we'd rather be, we head to leave the ground early just as Coventry Sphinx add a sixth goal from the penalty spot. The faint bursts of the whistle in the distance signify the game is over as we head on to the street that takes us back towards the train station, to head back to Leamington and the pub.

Still, though, I can't complain with how the day's gone. I'm drunk and feeling good, sadly a rare combination in the latter half of that second year at university. The day has been spent with good friends, the sort of company a lot of people yearn for. Most importantly, today has been the day I can finally be sure that I'm fully over Georgina, and the mental state I was in a couple of years ago. God knows I needed to feel that. All there is to do now is enjoy what's left of the weekend, on a night out in a town full of great pubs and great people.

The remaining hours, though, are fleeting, and it's not as though you can pretend coronavirus is not a thing. Social distancing regulations mean there's a queue for the Wetherspoons that stretches far down the high street, meaning the first pub of the planned crawl is written off immediately. The next two have exactly the same problem, and it's over an hour until we get into a pub at all, a trip we make via a takeaway, as there's no way we'll find somewhere doing food as well as booze. The second we do eventually get sat down, the news filters through – Britain will be going back into a month-long lockdown. Among many other things, grassroots football will be put on hold until 2 December. Beyond this point, who knows what will happen?

Suddenly the night out doesn't have quite the same feeling of freedom that it normally might. There's the sense of a clock ticking down: three hours until you're locked away for a month... two... one. The laughter is manufactured, the smiles forced. Paradoxically, there's a feeling that you've got to be having a good time to make the most of the time you have left, but this fact makes it impossible to do so. As I sit there with yet another drink, I ponder over the situation for lower-league football. The season is meant to be finished by June, and the games are already crammed in due to the late September start. This lockdown will cause problems, and if it is extended, that might be the final nail in the coffin. There would be no exciting title races, or relegation battles. There would be no Wembley final, no team of local heroes strutting out at the national stadium for the day of their lives, in what would be the day of the lives of many townspeople too. Everything is up in the air. It stopped raining hours ago, but now a dark cloud hangs overhead as the night grinds to its untimely demise.

5

Sutton Common Rovers vs Southall

6 December 2020

THE BEAUTIFUL game went for over a month with nobody in attendance, before the grim streak was ultimately broken last Wednesday as the nationwide lockdown finally ended. The 'elite' of the National League North and South upwards plodded on, but like the proverbial tree in the forest nobody has been there to hear or see it. In 30 years' time, you'll have conspiracy theorists arguing that Salford's stoppage-time equaliser at Harrogate, which allowed them to sneak into the play-off places, was faked, created on CGI by a desperate computer designer held at gunpoint by Gary Neville. There are some positives to the blanket ban on spectators, though: sitting at home watching a stream of Sutton United get hammered 4-0 at Wrexham made me incredibly grateful for the fact that I wasn't there, and could quietly turn off my laptop and go to bed as the fourth goal went in rather than having a four-hour journey home to stew over things.

It had also been over a month up until Wednesday since I'd left the house to do anything other than walk the dog or go to the shops, usually at the same time. I've struggled to find any sort of positives to this particular issue. It got to the point where the highlight of the week was the Tuesday Greggs delivery I get to reward myself for making it through my lunchtime meeting. I was in bed by ten most nights, not because I needed the sleep but because I simply had nothing to stay up for. It wasn't much of an entertaining existence, or a particularly healthy one for that matter.

When the release from lockdown eventually came, then, I was certainly relieved, but to be perfectly honest, not a lot has actually changed. With London now in tier two, the rules on getting a drink at a pub are so complex that you might as well need to recite a secret code to get a pint. Half the country doesn't even have pubs at all, or indeed a lot else for that matter. The tier three areas are in lockdown in all but name, and the fact the hotels in Middlesbrough are all closed put paid to the plan of heading back up north for the weekend to visit Grandad. He has been dealing with the situation by hosting a couple of mates on the days they'd usually head down to the social club in Stockton, and I really don't blame him. Yes, it's technically illegal, but what else can you do?

All this lockdown stuff has unsurprisingly been causing havoc with the FA Vase as well. All games after the last round were postponed indefinitely, with new dates to be found when the picture became clearer. With things staying more than a bit murky in that sense, they were lumped on consecutive weekends immediately after lockdown was to end, in order to catch up. The trouble is, tier three rules state clubs have to play behind closed doors, taking away virtually all of their income. Leagues in affected areas opted to stay suspended, whereas other leagues in tier one and tier two were able to keep going. The FA were uncompromising over the Vase, though, with all games to take place as planned only a week before. Does that all make sense to you? Nope, me neither.

Half the sides playing therefore ended up with no league fixtures to prepare them, and would be making financial losses from having nobody there to see them. There have even been calls recently on social media for all clubs involved to pull out and show the FA up, though somebody quite reasonably pointed out the FA probably wouldn't care, as there isn't any money involved in the Vase anyway. In the end, only three clubs heeded the call – Burton Park Wanderers, Mildenhall Town and Kirkley & Pakefield withdrawing from the competition before the second round was due to begin.

While football in non-league's lower tiers descends into farce in the background, there's been good news for Sutton United, though. Quite unexpectedly, the government decided a couple of weeks back that fans would be allowed back into grounds for elite football, starting from this weekend. In a matter of days, the outlook swings from not being able to see my team live until next season to being able to attend the Solihull Moors fixture on 5 December. The days at work miraculously start to drag by a lot more, but eventually the day arrives.

Throughout everything that has hit me in life, football has always been the one constant, guaranteeing that whatever is going on in the week, there will always be something to look forward to at the end of it. Even during that tough period in my second year of university, I travelled to every single game, using it as something of a break from reality. Even though my break-up with Georgina coincided with Sutton's catastrophic loss of form, just the fact I was out of the house and shouting myself hoarse at something else was enough to get me through. Typically, the summer months are the longest months of the year for me. May is manageable with the odd cup final on, and the play-offs to keep an eye on as well, getting to see which new places I'll get to visit with my team, but June is always like swimming through treacle. Pre-season in July is like your mum saying you're having pizza for dinner and then getting an Aldi value one out of the freezer, but after a month of no football at all it's always a blessed relief. Going nine months without my only real form of escapism was unfathomable to me.

Two hundred and 65 days. That's how long it's been since I last met my mates in the pub before the game, had a few drinks, and then walked down the high street to cut through Collingwood Rec and sauntered through the home turnstile with five minutes until kick-off; 265 days since the last furious shout towards the ref, imploring him to give you something, anything; 265 days since the last goal and the wild celebrations that follow it, leading into the jubilant singing as your side start to assert a level of control. I'm almost slightly concerned I won't know how to react to anything any more.

Frustratingly, this coveted fixture falls on the same weekend as the next round of FA Vase fixtures. For a few hours, the trade-off between being there for the first Sutton United game with fans back or continuing on my mission to make each round of the Vase eats away at me. On one side, I've committed to this, and I'm enjoying it, but I can't miss the first Sutton game in so long. There's a solution, though, and it lies very close to home indeed. Sutton Common Rovers, tenants at Sutton United's Gander Green Lane, ply their trade in the Combined Counties League, the London and Surrey representation in the ninth tier. They're still in the competition, in fact they have had a bye to this stage after their strong performance last year, and have been given a home draw. With United's game against Solihull obviously taking precedence, Sutton Common Rovers are due to play their tie on the Sunday afternoon. Having not been to Gander Green Lane for the football since March, I'll be going twice in 24 hours.

The Saturday game is an absolute dream. Two first-half goals put us in control, and despite a wobble at the start of the second half we get two more brilliant goals to win 4-1 against one of the title favourites. The day runs smoothly despite the plethora of restrictions that now exist; everyone follows the rules and it feels safe. Even the celebrations after the goals are reined in a bit, a particularly tough ask after backup right-back Aaron Simpson's rocket into the top corner from all of 25 yards. The best part of the day, though, is simply catching up with everyone again, all in the same place and all sharing a common interest. Football clubs are often described as the centre of the community, but it's clear to see more than ever now. Some of these guys I've been in touch with most days still, despite the lockdown, but others I haven't seen since March. Life gets in the way sometimes, but football often transcends life.

It goes without saying, but among the crowd on Saturday is Dan, probably the person I've stayed in touch with the most while we've all been stuck in lockdown. His frustrations over the last month or so have been exactly the same as mine, and it doesn't take much convincing for him to decide he'll come along to tomorrow's game as well. It's fair to say that, all in all, Saturday sets the bar for Sunday very high indeed.

Prior to going to the FA Vase game on Sunday, there's the small matter of Sunday league to deal with, a fixture against top-of-the-table Teddington Athletic providing the challenge this time. For once, I'm not hungover, having specifically avoided drinking after yesterday's victory. I'd like to say it's because the whole experience of being back watching Sutton United was so good I didn't need to drink, but that would be a bit of a lie. If I'm honest, it's because I've already played against Teddington Athletic earlier in the season, and their striker, a massive grafter called Deano, absolutely bullied me. We lost 6-0, and with five of those goals coming in the first half we were probably quite lucky it wasn't worse. Since then, we've failed to pick up a single point, though at least we've improved slightly since our 11-0 hammering on the opening day.

Deano is the least of my worries today, though. As a new side, we're always allocated the worst pitches at the worst times, and today is no different. A 12.45pm start over at Wimbledon Common Extensions, not exactly local to Sutton, means we're going to be tight for time if we want to make the start of the Sutton Common game. Somewhat predictably, the game is over as a contest long before half-time, and eventually, after another 6-0 defeat with Deano bagging another hat-trick, me and Dan jump in the car to speed across to Gander Green Lane as quickly as we can.

Typically, though, there is yet again a traffic light conspiracy against us as we watch the clock tick by. Every single set of lights, of which there are ludicrously many, suddenly turn red as we approach. The same cyclist overtakes us about 20 times as we get brought to a juddering halt every few hundred metres. The result is, we don't pull into the surprisingly busy car park until a quarter past three, the game already well under way.

Fortunately, we don't seem to have missed anything, the large scoreboard at the far end of the ground showing that the game is still goalless as we have our temperatures taken on entry. It promises to be a bit of a cracker today, with Sutton Common top of their league and their opponents for the day, Southall, not far behind. Moving to groundshare at Gander Green Lane has really been the making of this Sutton Common side. They started off as a Sunday league club back in 1978, taking sponsorships from a variety of pubs, leading to glorious names such as SCR Litten Tree and SCR Plough. It wasn't until 2004 that they moved into Saturday football at all, and it took them another four years to reach the Combined Counties League. This brought challenges in itself, with ground-grading regulations meaning they had to move to Leatherhead and then Cobham to find somewhere to play, changing their name to Mole Valley SCR as a result. They became something of a yo-yo side, moving between the Premier and First divisions of the Combined Counties League, before finally moving back to Sutton in 2015. Since then, they've turned their fortunes around to look like genuine title challengers, which would result in promotion to the highest level they've ever played at.

They look a good side as soon as we get in, to be fair, passing the ball around nicely on the artificial surface, though without looking particularly threatening. Southall largely look to just keep their shape and frustrate the hosts, whose first chance typically comes after I've gone to the tea hut to get some cheesy chips, desperate to fill myself up after another tough Sunday morning encounter. The ground still shows signs of the big occasion yesterday, with sauce packets and napkins strewn across the terraces. Being the home of a side four divisions above this level, Gander Green Lane is one of the biggest grounds at which you can expect to see an FA Vase tie played until the showpiece event at Wembley. There's a mix of old and new, the grandstand outdating Sutton Common as a club by almost 30 years, while the new Rec End terrace, brought right up against the pitch, is only a few years old. With banks of terracing virtually the whole way round, there's plenty of places to get a good view, and there's a decent crowd in today to take advantage of that.

Dan and I, still covered in mud, smelling awful, and wearing only tracksuits over our soaking wet football kits, understandably opt to stand as far away from anyone else as physically possible.

Sutton Common, wearing the same shade of yellow as their landlords, get their noses in front after a surprisingly good bit of work from the referee, of all people. A quick break forward is halted by a cynical tackle, which is such an obvious foul that the Southall players themselves stop and wait for the free kick to be given. The referee puts his whistle to his mouth, but just as he's about to blow, he spots another attacking player coming through and plays advantage. Adam Allen can't believe his luck and calmly slots home as the Southall players stand around looking accusatorially at each other.

Rather than reacting positively to this blow, Southall only seem to sit deeper and invite more pressure on to themselves. Their supporters, who are in good numbers, do not look particularly impressed. A couple of blokes standing behind a flag shake their heads as they look on, while an old boy with a red and white rosette opts to head over to the tea hut as the game goes on behind him, already looking somewhat resigned.

While Sutton Common Rovers were still bouncing around the South London Sunday League scene, Southall actually reached the final of the FA Vase back in 1986. Despite having a young Les Ferdinand up top, they ended up well beaten by Halesowen Town, and never really managed to hit those heights again. A lack of interest in the side meant Southall had to move out of their ground in 1992, not being able to afford the upkeep, and the club have been nomadic since. Things have been looking up over the last few years, though, with the team playing their best football since the turn of the century and plans for a new ground finally afoot. Today, though, it looks like they'd do very well to channel any of that optimism as Sutton Common Rovers continue to surge all over them.

As the old man wearing the rosette hands over his change and picks up his cup of coffee, Sutton Common are awarded a free kick more than 25 yards from goal. It's sufficiently far out for nobody from the away side to really look too worried as Danny Fernandez steps up. It's hit true, though, and clears the wall before dipping viciously over the hand of the Southall keeper. Sickeningly, the ball crashes off the underside of the crossbar and away from goal, with Fernandez briefly looking gutted. However, Southall's defence resembles a game of musical statues once again and there's nobody in the same postcode as Kyle Henry, who has all the time in the world to head the loose ball into a now unguarded net. Sutton Common Rovers lead 2-0 with ten minutes to go until half-time.

As the players make their way back to the centre circle, there's a bit of argy-bargy and a few players on each side seem to square up to each other. The Southall number seven is adamant something has happened, screaming, 'What's he doing, what's he doing?' to the ref over and over again. We're stood completely over the opposite side of the pitch to the dugouts but can still clearly hear the Sutton Common manager shout 'fucking walk away' at about 1,000 decibels as things get heated. The stadium announcer seemingly panics and plays Pulp's 'Common People' over the tannoy for no apparent reason, making for quite a comical scene as the players involved are eventually pulled away from each other. Barely 30 seconds after the restart, the angry-looking Southall number four puts in a horror tackle on the very player he'd squared up to just a minute ago, and is duly sent off. The rest of his team-mates carry looks of frustration that suggest he's done this before as he heads off down the tunnel without looking back. Game over.

As the first half starts to peter out, conversation between me and Dan moves bizarrely towards Britain's Eurovision entry. We're both convinced that with no chance of ever winning anyway, we might as well enter a group of Sutton United fans singing the popular terrace song about the size of midfielder Kenny Davis's penis. It's a motion that would certainly attract a fair bit of support in this neck of the woods.

Dan had developed something of a Eurovision obsession during his university years, with the final streamed annually on the big screen in the Student Union Piazza. Despite the cult crowds and carnival atmosphere, it was probably the one aspect of student life I was happy to miss out on, with the musical standard often around the level of the student karaoke the following evening.

While on holiday at the less-than-idyllic Spanish coastal resort of Lloret de Mar last year, we came across a karaoke bar where Celine Dion was particularly popular with the non-English speakers. Researching one of her songs after a particularly poor rendition by some screechy French girls, Dan was shocked to discover that she'd won the 1988 Eurovision Song Contest for Switzerland, despite not being Swiss. To make matters worse, the UK had only been beaten to the title by a singular point that year, before the rest of Europe hated us. Furiously, and indeed quite drunkenly, Dan posted on his Facebook account to wish everyone except the Swiss a good evening. Sadly, he forgot his line manager at his summer internship was of the nationality. He wasn't offered a full-time role there when the summer was up.

Moving round to stand behind the goal Sutton Common are attacking in the second half gives a rather strange view of the terrace up the other side. Half of the curved bank looks clean, while the other half is still caked in years' worth of dirt. This might appear a mystery to the average person, admittedly probably not one they'd lose any sleep over, but me and Dan share a knowing smile as we look across. Over the summer, the club appealed for volunteers to help with the ground maintenance. Among other various tasks, we answered their call by bringing along a pressure washer and setting to work on a job that is a hell of a lot harder, and more boring, than it looks. Unfortunately, a few weeks into the task, I tested positive for coronavirus, and by the time I got out of self-isolation we never really regained the momentum to finish the job. The evidence of our ultimate laziness is still clearly visible to this day.

Given that we've changed ends of the ground to be closer to the action, it's typical that instead it's Southall who start much the brighter of the two sides in the second half. The home goalkeeper might as well have brought a deckchair along for the first half, but within five minutes of the restart he's called upon twice to keep his team's two-goal lead intact. The travelling supporters don't seem particularly buoyed by this, though, restricting their appreciation to a polite round of applause every now and then. Sutton Common's lively winger is more animated than this, screaming 'WHAT THE FUCK IS THIS SHIT?' for all his team-mates, the supporters and the rest of the population of the London Borough of Sutton to hear. His anger does the trick, though, and the home side soon regain control, making good use of the extra space they now have with Southall a man down.

The standout performer for the away side without a doubt is their goalkeeper, Lewis Todd. As Sutton Common up the ante and start to pepper his goal more and more, he seems to rise to the challenge, relishing the opportunity to prove himself. With each save he makes, he seems to grow in stature, filling the goal even more, proving the last block against what would otherwise probably end up a cricket score. He can't do anything about the third goal on the hour mark, though, Kyle Henry again on hand to tap home from close range. Henry is the left winger but has a poacher's touch that most strikers at this level would die for, and whenever the ball is in the box he's never far away. Dan tips him for a hat-trick, which of course means he's inevitably subbed off five minutes later instead.

This doesn't stop the onslaught, and a fourth goal only minutes after the change is only stopped by the linesman's flag. Sutton Common's right-back doesn't spot it, though, and awkwardly gives a loud cry of celebration in an otherwise silent stadium. An embarrassing moment of my own follows soon after when a cross drifts over the goal and into the section of the terrace of which Dan and I are the sole occupants. Instinctively, I go to head it back, but my form from this morning's Sunday league game carries through and it's badly miscued further away from the pitch. Thankfully, the referee awards a dubious corner and takes the attention away from me in the process.

'Give us a chance, ref, we've only got nine men,' one of the Southall players complains. Hang on a second. NINE men? A quick count of the remaining players on the pitch confirms it. It's no wonder it's been so one-sided then. The next step is trying to work out how and when it happened. Looking at Twitter confirms our suspicions – a Southall player was shown a straight red card inside the opening ten minutes, before Dan's battered Renault Clio had made it over from our Sunday morning match. Having the luxury of the scoreboard to tell us the score meant we didn't bother checking if anything else had happened; after all, you don't really expect a sending-off inside ten minutes, though perhaps after the games I've seen in previous rounds it's not that much of a shock. That makes seven red cards in four rounds now, even if I've only actually seen six of them.

Now that we've finally realised what's going on, the continued domination of Sutton Common over one of their league title challengers makes more sense. The pessimism of the travelling supporters is more understandable, the fury of the home side's winger early in the second half more justified. It also means that when Southall miss a sitter to get a goal back, Dan is even more critical of the lax defending that allows them a free header six yards from goal.

By now, Dan has lost interest, though: he's an Arsenal fan, and the north London derby against Tottenham has already kicked off. I promised him earlier that we could head to the pub slightly early to catch as much of the game as possible, but our position on the covered terrace means we can't see the scoreboard, and I can happily lie about the time until there's only seconds to go. I know if we do leave early we'll miss something, but agree to finally walk round to leave as the game enters added time. As we get into the car, a loud shout arises from the ground, and another check of Twitter confirms Sutton Common have added a fourth right at the death. Just as I'm having a go at Dan, Arsenal go a goal down. I have to admit, it makes me feel a little better.

Secret code successfully recited, we make it into the pub and get drinks under the claim that we're a bubble, whatever that's supposed to mean. Arsenal lose, but it still doesn't kill the mood as Dan and I look to make the most of the two allocated hours we have to drink with our meal.

It's not quite normal as such, and the phrase 'new normal' does nothing but piss me off, but it's still such a blessed relief after the last four weeks, and indeed the last seven or so months. Many people have said it, but I've definitely been guilty of taking simple things like playing Sunday league or going to the pub, even watching my beloved Sutton United, for granted. They're activities which have new value now, and the dry period of the peak of lockdown has forced me to find basic value in other things. It might sound a bit idealistic, but if there was ever a time to look for the positives, this is it.

6

Malvern vs Sporting Khalsa

19 December 2020

HAVE YOU ever considered your football obsession to have gone too far? Perhaps you've made a ten-hour round journey on a Tuesday night to see your hopeless side beaten 4-0. Maybe you live hundreds of miles away from your side's home ground but still regularly make the trip down to games. In all likelihood, you've probably had a standoff about it with the other half at some stage, and I hope you didn't back down. I've done something along the lines of all of those, but when I leave my house at 5.30am in the pissing rain to head to Malvern Town vs Sporting Khalsa in the FA Vase, I feel like even for me this could be a new low.

There are plenty of mitigating circumstances, in fairness. My brother is back from university, where he's picked up a new girlfriend in his first term. Understandably, they don't want to be apart for the next few months, so it's agreed that they're going to live together. Unfortunately, this is at our house. A building that was initially designed with two bedrooms now has six people living in it, with predictably painful results. In more ways than one, I'm getting a *Big Brother* experience now, and it's miserable. I even have to leave the house through the back door in the mornings to avoid disturbing them asleep in the front room before they get up at around midday, every single day. Their late starts aren't surprising given that they get home in the early hours most nights, somehow finding something to do despite the virtual lockdown we're in. I know the times they get in, because they wake me up most nights. I'm at the point of praying Exeter University allow their students back soon.

Now the 5.30am start probably makes a bit more sense to you. A full day out of the house is desperately needed, and Malvern is the perfect location. I've not just picked it for the football, with the beauty of the Malvern Hills dominating the landscape. My train gets in early enough to climb them too, and with Louis from my old university house able to jump on at Oxford on the way through, I've got company. With lockdown none too thrilling for him, either, Louis is also grateful for the escape. As the train finally winds through the countryside and up to the town, though, and the majestic scenery appears in the window, his enthusiasm wavers slightly, 'Jesus, is that the fucking hill?'

At its highest point, 425 metres above sea level, with drizzling rain falling on the steep slopes and a bitter cold permeating the air, I can see why it would be imposing to somebody wearing Adidas trainers and a lightweight hoodie, who's also drinking a can of Budweiser before 10am. Still, the task is to climb it and get back down again all before the match starts, something we've planned to absolutely no level whatsoever. It's a case of just head upwards and hope for the best really. If worst comes to worst, maybe we can watch the game from the top of the Worcestershire Beacon, the highest point of the landscape for miles around. The one bit of preparation we can do at this stage is getting a full English breakfast, which allows me to charge my phone up slightly as well. To be honest, there's not really much point. The phone is almost as old as the hills themselves, and in the cold the battery lasts about ten minutes if you're lucky. I can check the route inside the cafe as the waitress shuffles about awkwardly on what's clearly her first shift, but once we're up on the hill we're on our own.

Since I last saw Louis, at the Coventry Sphinx game on the eve of the last lockdown in October, he's made little progress on his job hunt. Numerous online assessment centres have been and gone, but without reward. Quite frankly, he's doing well to even be getting that far with the way the world is at the minute. With virtually no part-time work available, either, life is somewhat standing still for one of my best mates. It's no easier on the social side of things, either. With his dad being in the shielding category, every time Louis comes in from a night out he has to head straight to his room, take a test and wait for a negative result before he can come out again, meaning a day out like this is effectively two days out of the schedule. An asthmatic himself, and currently nursing a back injury, it's fair to say hill climbing probably isn't his ideal choice of activity, but I didn't need to ask him twice when I first told him of my plans. Any escape these days is a win, and not just for me.

Mindful of the fact we actually want to get to the match later, we start the climb with haste, powering past an old couple who must be well into their 80s. This gives us a great sense of achievement, until we have to stop for breath about two minutes later and are embarrassingly overtaken by the two pensioners chuckling at us not too subtly. Amazingly, we do actually make reasonable progress after this first steep stretch, despite the challenges that coming off the concrete path poses. Each step is a potential disaster, the winter mud lying in wait around every corner. My Adidas Hamburgs don't offer much grip and there are a few near-misses, but we make it to within sight of the top with no disasters. At this point, Louis takes control of the route, his second can of lager bringing out the confidence in his Duke of Edinburgh-learned navigation skills, and we cut away from the paths altogether to go cross-country on a new express route to the top. Against all reason and logic, it works, and less than an hour from setting off we're on top of the world.

The cliché would be to describe the top, and the sense of achievement, as a moment of peace. The truth is anything but. The wind howls aggressively, and we stagger about trying to stay on our two feet as if we've had ten pints each to drink rather than just Louis having two. As we do this, we're snared by a dog lead as a woman walking four yappy terriers takes her eye off them for a second. Despite this, it's still brilliant, and Louis's initial cynicism has completely disappeared as he beams from ear to ear. The view from the top is generally considered to be one of the best in Britain, and on what has now become a bright and sunny day you can fully understand why. The weak sun filters down through the atmosphere, bathing the route across the hills in a heavenly gold light. The town looks like an idyllic model village, complete with church spire rising up above quaint little houses. You can even see the football ground from our vantage point. There's a lot of people about, pretty much all in proper climbing gear, with us two the only exception, and it's only now that I start to really get it. The task of getting to the top takes your mind off everything else, and the feeling at the top is a little bit like the warm feeling after picking up three points. Get something that could recreate celebrating a goal and I'd almost be tempted to join the club on a more regular basis.

With the way the world is at the minute, I would be surprised if I was the only one tempted by the outdoor lifestyle. The importance of getting yourself out of the house has never been clearer to me, and the government can't really stop you doing that, no matter how bad it gets. Not even slipping flat on my arse three times on the way down can take the smile off my face, simply because I've managed to do something other than sit and stare at a screen all day. My head feels clearer, my life more fulfilled. With the main event of the football still to come, it promises to be a good day, one of few good days I've had in the last year or so.

After earlier fears of not making the start of the match at all, it's refreshing that we manage to get back down to the bottom of the hill with more than an hour to while away in the pub before kick-off. With a plug socket available, it also gives me the chance to bring my phone back to life, but this is something I regret almost the instant the screen flashes back on again. It's a moment of real déjà vu – the news states that Boris Johnson is to address the country later today, with rumours of yet another lockdown. The misery of the evening of the Coventry Sphinx game a couple of months ago crops up fresh in my mind again. I turn my phone back off. If only I was still up that hill; if only I could be there indefinitely until all this shit was over.

What's more, I'm trying to stay off the booze as much as possible today with a big day ahead tomorrow. My Sunday league side, still bottom on zero points, come up against the side almost as awful as us. Given our combined goal difference of -62 from 12 games, it's probably our only chance of picking up points this season, so I've got to be on top form. Unsurprisingly, a Wetherspoons at lunchtime with a drunken mate isn't quite so much fun when you're stone-cold sober. To cap it all off, I suppose there's a chance the game tomorrow might not even go ahead now. With that in mind, I order a double rum and Coke to try and drink away at least some of the bleakness starting to engulf me.

If not at the top of a hill with no internet, being at a football match in the FA Vase is probably the second-best thing for getting away from all this misery, and I'm expecting big things from the game today. Malvern Town are the underdogs, playing their league football in the Hellenic League Division One West alongside the likes of Hereford Lads Club and Tytherington Rocks. The standard might not be the best, but Malvern are top of the table with ten wins from 11 games, and it won't be an easy task for their opponents. Sporting Khalsa are top of the Midland Football League Premier Division, the tier above Malvern. With just one defeat in what is a very strong division, Khalsa might easily be considered one of the favourites for the entire tournament, never mind this match. As they say, though, you never quite know in cup football.

Malvern have already been one of the stories of the previous round. They faced Atherstone Town, another tenth-tier side, and beat them 1-0. Doesn't sound like too much, right? Go back to last season, though, and the two teams were also drawn together, at the same stage of the competition Malvern are at now. A far cry from this season's close battle, Atherstone absolutely battered Malvern 10-0. Even weirder, that came after a replay, the original tie finishing 3-3. It's anyone's guess as to what Malvern were doing that night.

The game today is a sell-out, and we've had to be on our toes to secure tickets, which is something of a novelty for an FA Vase third-round tie. As Louis walks in, he's asked if he's a home or an away fan, a question that causes him some difficulty given he's had more than a few beers and we're technically neither. The man on the gate isn't too concerned by our neutral status, though, and explains they've got to have some sort of segregation in place. It's as simple as asking Sporting Khalsa fans to turn right instead of left as they enter, but it does just about do the job, I suppose. The ground has recently had a 3G pitch installed, and what was previously a large grass area adjacent to three sides of the pitch has now been fenced off, with only a small spectator area remaining. There's plenty of room, though, and with the weather we've had recently, the loss of the grass spectator area is probably for the best. Indeed, the 'mud spectator area' would probably be a better description at this point.

Malvern walk out in their claret and blue to a reception that suggests they're probably not expected to get any further in the competition. The applause is rapturous, but the shouts of encouragement that accompany it are hopeful more than anything else. Khalsa enter the pitch calmly, their small band of supporters in the corner of the ground barely noticeable. A quiet day at the office is the best outcome for them today, progressing to the next round without having to make much of a fight of it. If they do want to get to the Wembley final, they'll face much tougher tests on paper, and they know that. For the home side, this assignment is about as tough as it gets.

The game is barely five minutes old when disaster strikes for Malvern. A low cross into the box is sliced under pressure by a nervy-looking centre-back, the ball spinning off his foot and beating the stunned keeper at his near post. With the laser-flat artificial surface, there's no excuses, and the Khalsa players look almost too embarrassed by it to celebrate. If today was a tough ask for Malvern before kick-off, it certainly isn't any easier now. It would be easy for heads to drop, and to be honest, I expect the worst, but instead of going quiet, the voices on the pitch are ramped up even more. Led by their commanding captain, Louis Loader, there's never a danger that they might lose heart. In fact, they probably even start to get the upper hand as Khalsa let the tempo drop slightly.

With the background to the stadium so impressive, I spend half the time trying to get a nice picture rather than paying particularly close attention to the game. I have the good sense to look up when the home side come close from a corner, though, and then as a breakaway is crudely halted in a dangerous-looking wide position. The resulting free kick is well delivered, the header won by a man in claret and blue, and the ball moves towards goal. From where we're standing, it's hard to tell exactly what's happening. The ball hits the post and moves across goal, but it's the goal the Sporting Khalsa fans are meant to be behind. With the travelling support not exactly packing out their section, there's literally nobody there. The home fans up our end don't react until after the players wheel away to celebrate – Malvern have equalised.

Having reacted so well to going behind, the underdogs start to thrive after their equaliser. It reminds me of Aston Villa's shock 7-2 win over Liverpool in the Premier League earlier in the season. When Malvern pour forward, they do it with purpose, pace, aggression, and Khalsa at times don't really know what to do. On many an occasion, they're saved by an offside flag when otherwise one of the wingers would be in on goal. Eventually, they get one where the flag stays down, and Harry Clark gets in down the left side. The crowd holds its breath, but Clark strokes it home with the nonchalance of a playground kickabout to send everyone wild. Bizarrely, one of the more drunken fans behind the goal shouts 'next goal wins' with no context or explanation at all.

You could understand the home side sitting back on their lead, trying to slow the pace a little now they're unexpectedly ahead, but they do nothing of the sort. Khalsa look shell-shocked, and struggle to get their main men into the game to any effect.

Sporting Khalsa are a club with an interesting story. Based in Willenhall, between Walsall and Wolverhampton, the club was set up in 1991 by the local Sikh community and has progressed from Sunday league to the Midland Football League. Since reaching the ninth tier in 2015, they've regularly challenged for promotion, and were right in the mix last season before the outbreak of coronavirus cruelly rendered the season null and void, negating their efforts. There is no requirement for the players to be British Asian; indeed, the majority aren't, but the Sikh community does have some representation. Gurjit 'Gaz' Singh is well known in West Midlands non-league circles for being one of the most prolific strikers around. His form at Khalsa's level, though for other sides including Smethwick and Tipton Town, got him a move to Kidderminster in the National League. Though he did well there, he has since gradually dropped back down the pyramid, joining Khalsa initially in 2018 before re-signing at the start of the 2019/20 season after a brief spell away. Sporting Khalsa's website gives an interesting take on the striker on his player profile, 'Gaz says it breaks his heart how the Kardashian and Jenner ladies always seem to have such rotten luck with the men they fall in love with.'

That's not the only thing breaking his heart today as the Malvern Town defence repeatedly shuts him out of the game. A man with such a fine goalscoring record is surely on paper the main threat, but he can't be much of a threat if he never touches the ball. Half an hour in, the home side are still on top, and I'm struggling to think of a single time Singh has even had a kick. As this thought crosses my mind, he's picked out by a good pass on the edge of the box and weaves cleverly away from two defenders to get a shot off. It's hit with venom, and the next thing anyone knows about it is when it smacks the fence behind the goal, having only cleared the post by an inch or two. It's a warning sign, but luckily for Malvern no more than that.

Just minutes later, I turn away from another poor attempt at getting a scenic shot of the ground to see Harry Clark through on goal again. If it was on TV, I might have thought I was watching a replay of the second goal, such is the similarity as the right side of Sporting Khalsa's defence seems to go completely missing. Having found the corner the first time, Clark goes through the keeper's legs this time with exactly the same result as, incredibly, Malvern go 3-1 up. The way the game has gone, it doesn't feel like a smash and grab or a shock at all, though. The tenth-tier side have been playing with confidence, pressing high and knocking the ball around well on the artificial surface. Another goal while this dominance lasts and they should definitely be able to see it over the line. Khalsa finally seem to wake up at this point, but there isn't long until half-time, and they can't reduce the deficit before the break. The way both sides have played, the shock is very much on the cards.

Perhaps unsurprisingly, Khalsa make two changes at half-time as they desperately try to force their way back into the game. Singh is one of the two replaced, that powerful long-range shot not enough to save him from the humiliation of the half-time axe. The changes don't help, though, and Malvern continue to dominate against all the odds. The main problem Khalsa had in the first half was allowing the Malvern wingers far too much space, and it's only three minutes into the second half when the home side's other winger, Joe Bates, gets into acres once more. By the time the defender can get across, he's able to set himself perfectly for the shot, and the power takes it past the luckless keeper to make it 4-1. The home fans behind the goal where I'm now standing can't believe it. Surely now that's it.

I remark to Louis that I would have had Sporting Khalsa down as one of the favourites for the whole tournament, to which his response is, 'Think again, mate.' My response of 'not yet' is met with derisory laughter. Nothing seems to be going Khalsa's way, not least when the keeper looks to kick the ball over to where a throw-in is due to be taken but succeeds only in hitting his own player in the face. The jeers from the crowd can probably be heard from the other side of Worcestershire. On another occasion, he turns to the crowd as he picks up his water bottle. 'Keeper,' shouts a lone voice from a metre away, waiting for a response. 'You're shit.' The rest of the home fans burst into laughter as if they've just heard a top-of-the-range one-liner as opposed to the most basic put-down in the book.

Malvern come forward again, Bates gets in down the channel again, and suddenly there's a chance for a fifth. It's ridiculous just how easily Sporting Khalsa's defence keep making the same mistakes over and over again, but this time the keeper is there to save them, and the rebound is cleared off the line. With the sun setting over the hills that dominate the backdrop, you might say Sporting Khalsa have a mountain to climb.

With the pedigree in their side, though, they're not about to give up just yet. Just after the hour mark, a bullet header makes it 4-2, and it's game on. Khalsa rush the ball back to the centre circle, eager to get going again, fully believing the game is still in their hands. Malvern take the kick, play it back to a defender and then knock it back into midfield straight away. The midfielder turns and plays a pass forward through the middle. Having spent the entire game unable to defend the wings, Khalsa mix it up a little by going completely absent in the centre of defence, and Joe Bates can't quite believe it as he bears down on goal. The keeper comes out, takes him down, and the ref points to the spot. We've been playing for less than ten seconds since the restart. Having let their opponents back into the game, this is the chance to put them back out of it again straight away.

Matt Turner steps up looking confident, and the crowd feels surprisingly relaxed. Louis has already declared the game over again, and the home fans seem to share his confidence. Turner steps up and scuffs his kick straight down the middle. The keeper doesn't move. It's one of the easiest saves he'll ever make. As he celebrates with his team-mates and Turner stands and looks dejected, you feel that this could be the turning point. The cockiness of the crowd is no more, and you could hear a pin drop as the ball is played down the pitch. Let off the hook, Sporting Khalsa have got their tails up and look dangerous. Less than five minutes later, they've scored two more and the score is 4-4.

Nobody can quite believe it, myself included, as the small section of away fans is sent into delirium. The Khalsa goalkeeper, who has taken relentless stick all game, does not hold back as he celebrates in front of the Malvern fans gathered behind the goal. This time, there's no retort, no rebuttal. Khalsa get a corner, and as it's whipped in and met by the head of a yellow shirt, the away fans rise in celebration once more, only to have their joy cut short by an incredible goal-line clearance. Claims that the ball was already over the line when met by the head of Harry Clark, who's been busy at both ends today, fall on deaf ears. Malvern survive, for now. That's quite the thing to be saying about a side who had a three-goal lead so recently that you could have gone for a cup of tea and come back thinking it was still 4-1.

The game starts to slow down ever so slightly, though it has the feel of a boxer waiting for a final knockout punch after a slog of a bout. It's been an absolutely incredible encounter, possibly the best football match I've ever seen in all my years watching the sport. Nobody seems to mind as a sleeting rain starts to fall, adding to the bitter cold that has once again caused my phone to die. I'm convinced some people don't even notice. Having seen their side eventually weather the storm, the crowd start to creep out of their shells again, and roar into life when the Khalsa keeper miscontrols a simple pass and then has to punt the ball out for a corner. Perhaps they have a part to play, giving one final boost to a side that have given pretty much everything they've got. Both sides are tiring, and one Malvern defender deliberately hoofs his clearance miles out of the ground to get a precious few seconds' breather. It looks set for penalties, a cruel way to decide the game, but probably the only fair way of doing it. I've grown fond of Malvern and want them to win, but at the same time don't really want either side to lose. To think it only cost £6 to get in is ridiculous; it's arguably the best £6 I've ever spent.

Just as it looks as though both sides will accept their lottery fate, a ball forward out of nowhere finds Malvern's centre-forward in a good shooting position. Sporting Khalsa centre-back and St Kitts & Nevis international Tes Robinson takes no chances, absolutely clattering him with an elbow as he goes through on goal. The 35-year-old uses all his experience to make sure the foul is outside the box, but still expects the red card as he turns to the referee. However, the red card never comes, the ref opting for yellow instead. Furious accusations of 'bottler' are hurled at the man in black, but it won't make a difference. Oh well, there's only two minutes left anyway. What does it matter? The free kick is from one of those positions everyone says is too close to get over the wall and back down again, and those people would be absolutely right on this occasion. Louis Loader smacks it straight into the wall, but the wall is weak and the ball drops just the other side of it. Before anyone else can even comprehend what is happening, Harry Clark is on to it and smashes the ball into the back of the net to make it 5-4.

Oh. My. God. I can't find any words, just hysterical laughter. Even as a neutral, I've been dragged along on this emotional rollercoaster all afternoon, and there's been one final incredible twist. In fact, describing it as just a rollercoaster is an understatement. My excitement levels are probably as high as when I was on a rollercoaster at Thorpe Park aged 12 and a girl's boobs popped out. There's a bundle in the corner, social distancing goes out the window, but fuck it, anything goes. Football, fucking hell.

Rather than collapsing to the ground, though, Khalsa rush the ball back to the centre. To be fair, the way this game has gone, you wouldn't write anything off. Five minutes are added on: there's still time. Joy in the stands gives way to nerves, and then to terror every time the ball goes in the box. In all honesty, it's barely out of the box, corner after corner, long throw after long throw. When Malvern do eventually get the ball forward, they give a free kick away on the halfway line, allowing the ball to come straight back at them once more. A long ball is lofted in, and it's met by Tes Robinson, the man who should have been sent off just minutes earlier. From where we're standing, we see the ball loop to the far post. It's cleared off the line, but the Khalsa appeals are loud, louder than they've been for anything else today. Like an executioner with no qualms, the linesman raises his flag to indicate the ball has crossed the line. It's 5-5.

Before Malvern can even think about mourning their loss, Khalsa come forward again and get a throw-in, one that will be launched in again. We've played five minutes now – this will be it. I can barely watch as the ball is hurled into the box; I can't imagine what it would be like to be one of the players. It's only half-cleared and the ball falls to a Sporting Khalsa player on the edge of the box. As he lines up to hit it, with nobody within metres of him, the whole stadium, the whole town, holds its breath. It feels like an age but unfolds in only a couple of seconds in real time. With the keeper motionless, the ball thunders into the post and flies out across the box. A whole crowd of players throw themselves at it, half of them trying to force it in, half of them trying to force it away. The latter half comes out on top, and as the ball crosses the halfway line, the full-time whistle goes. I think I need to catch my breath almost as much as the players do.

'Whatever happens, lads, all the best,' says the Sporting Khalsa keeper, and the response he gets is one of genuine appreciation. It's such a shame one of these two sides has to go out today. Based on Malvern's awful penalty from the game itself, though, I fear it could well be them.

The penalties are to be taken at the end where we're standing, giving us a perfect view of what will now definitely be the final act of an extraordinary spectacle. After the warm exchange of a few moments ago, the Sporting keeper and Malvern fans are back to goading each other as Khalsa go 1-0 up. Malvern's first taker isn't the same bloke who took the penalty in the match, but he screws his effort painfully wide as the visitors celebrate. Already, this isn't looking good.

Khalsa score their second penalty, creating a huge amount of pressure already on the Malvern taker, who pretty much needs to score. Matt Turner, who missed the penalty earlier, steps up. This time he scores, and his sense of relief is palpable. Khalsa tuck their next couple away, and despite guessing the right way each time, the Khalsa keeper can't stop either of the Malvern penalties finding the back of the net, either. If Khalsa score their next kick, they're through. Stepping up to take it is Tes Robinson. It's impossible not to think back to the challenge he should have seen red for, and then his equalising goal just minutes later. This would really be rubbing salt into already catastrophic wounds if he tucks this away.

Malvern keeper Kieron Blackburn guesses right, though, and produces a strong block as the players on the halfway line go mad. There's a cry of 'justice' from one of the fans nearby, but Malvern still need to score to stay in it. Hat-trick hero Harry Clark is the man tasked with doing so. Thankfully, his goalscoring form continues and we go into sudden death, prolonging the excitement that bit longer. The first two penalties are arguably the best two in the whole shoot-out, but Khalsa's seventh taker, Josh

McKenzie, smiles a nervous smile as he places the ball on the spot. That smile turns to a look of horror before the ball even leaves his foot as he curls it high and wide, nearly taking out a kid sat on the railing as the ball bounces off the perimeter fence. For the first time in the shoot-out, Malvern have the chance to win it. Centre-back Adam Sauntson is the man with the unenviable task.

The result of this game doesn't affect me at all; I have no association with either side and in all likelihood won't see either play again, but I'm so nervous on Sauntson's behalf I can barely watch, let alone reply to Louis as he asks me what I think will happen. I hope to God he scores. I don't even want to consider what I think might happen. Sauntson himself looks relaxed. Up he steps, and crashes the ball home.

Now, finally, Malvern can celebrate properly, and celebrate they do. This time, there's no potential three-goal collapse or stoppage-time sting in the tail. Once the initial delirious scrum of players piled on top of Sauntson breaks up, chants of 'Wembley' are sung in unison by the players and fans together as the club photographer has an absolute field day, freezing those beaming smiles forever in time. The Malvern team are eventually given a hero's send-off down the tunnel, but not before the Sporting Khalsa players are given a standing ovation themselves by the home fans. If it wasn't for the pandemic, I'm sure the celebrations would be going on long into the night, and perhaps they will anyway, but Louis and I don't hang about to find out. Our train leaves town in half an hour, and my phone, which I've been using for navigation, is dead.

For all of Malvern's charm in the area near the hill itself, the football ground is on the other side of town and the streets all have the same nondescript look. Breaking the monotony of it all, a tractor covered in fairy lights drives past, a man dressed as Santa Claus sat in a trailer on the back shouting 'Merry Christmas' at the bewildered spectators leaving the ground. When I shout back to ask where the station is, neither Santa Claus nor his elf helper reply. Still drunk from earlier, Louis leads the way once more, hopefully as well as he did on our way up the hill. With the trains only every couple of hours, there hasn't been so much pressure on anyone since Adam Sauntson all of five minutes ago.

Riding our luck once more, we chance upon the railway bridge and just about manage to follow the roads back to the station itself from there. On the train, I can finally plug my phone in again and catch up on the day's events outside of Malvern as the notifications flood through. Good news of a Sutton United victory away at St Albans is soon forgotten when information that feels like a punch to the gut appears on screen.

In the time my phone has been blissfully dead since the pub, the government's press conference has taken place. London and the south-east are going into lockdown, yet again. I might just about be able to cope with this alone, but there's more. A new variant of coronavirus has been discovered in the UK, one that's significantly more infectious than the last. The best-case scenario is we'll be stuck in lockdown for a couple of months until the vaccination programme is rolled out. The worst case is that this new strain doesn't respond to the vaccine at all. In other words, there's no way out. Game over. And even in this best-case scenario, it isn't looking good for non-league football, the FA Vase included.

The outlook for the foreseeable future is bleak, to put it lightly. I'll be back at home, where I'll be stuck practically 24/7 with nothing to do but work. There will be no release to break the days up, nothing to look forward to at the end of the week. Undoubtedly, the awkward living situation at home will fan the flames of agitation, and if things do get out of control, there's nowhere to take refuge. Just to cap it all off, our Sunday league game tomorrow has been called off, and we'll be sat bottom of the table with no points for at least the next few months. I could have been drinking all day after all. I wish I had a drink now.

Having sat for most of the journey in silence, Louis gets off at Oxford to leave me alone with my own thoughts, which isn't a great place to be at the moment. It was all going so well, an enjoyable bit of outdoor activity followed by an absolute thriller of a football match. Yet with the breaking of one piece of news, my entire mood has changed. Being away from my phone for a day was great, but only because it delayed the inevitable. As the train crawls into Paddington, where hundreds of people wait to escape London and its impending lockdown, I wonder how I can prepare myself for this latest setback. To be honest, I wonder *if* I can.

7

Sutton Common Rovers vs Hadley

17 April 2021

THE LATEST lockdown has reminded me of the low points of my teenage years, times I don't exactly look back on with joy. It started at age 11, with checking everything was in my school bag at least ten times each night the morning before I was in, and making sure both of my cats were safely inside before I went to bed. This seemed innocent enough – 'he just cares about his schoolwork and loves his pets' – so nothing was done about it. It soon progressed to a fear of meeting new people, or even talking to the ones I vaguely knew. Phone calls were an absolute no-no; even speaking to family was something I would avoid at all costs. Before going out of the house, if I ever did, I needed to check every socket and light switch in the house to make sure there couldn't possibly be a fire, and push the door as if I was trying to break in to make sure nobody else could.

As the rest of my school year group progressed to attending house parties, I stayed very much at home. It wasn't that I didn't have friends, I had plenty, but I was terrified of going out. Every Friday evening I would train with my Sunday league team, every single one of whom was cooler than me. The conversation would start to be about girls, drinking, plans for the weekend, while I would hang awkwardly around the back of the group and try to speak as little as possible. The football part I loved, and I was good enough to get away with my awkwardness, but the social side was awful.

While my friends were out having fun, I would retreat to my safe zone, my bedroom, and sit and waste my life away, mostly playing *Football Manager*. I didn't see it as wasting away at the time, why would I? I didn't want to go out, so I didn't. I simply didn't fit in, and that was fine. I was happy anyway; going to the football at the weekend was enough for me. And that was my life: school in the weekdays and football at the weekend, nothing more. Eventually, I worked up the courage to go to my first house party, aged 17, to celebrate my Sunday league side becoming Surrey champions. I hated it. When I arrived, I watched the last half an hour of Norwich vs Middlesbrough on Sky while I got myself drunk enough to at least slightly calm the terror that engulfed me, telling whoever asked that I had a bet on the final score, to make myself look a bit less unusual, a bit less out of place. When the match finished, I'd never felt so alone. For maybe an hour and a half, I floated around saying the odd word to people I already knew before sneaking out of the back door and home to safety.

At university, I started to change a little, but only through an oppressive fear of missing out. I met people who I noticed were similar to me, and if they could do it so could I. Besides, I'd gotten pretty bored of *Football Manager* by now. It wasn't until my crisis visit to a counsellor two years later, after the Georgina break-up, that I was told my behaviour was consistent with anxiety. Hearing about the condition in that room that day, nothing had ever made so much sense at one time to me. I barely held it together until I was on my way home, eventually bursting into tears that threatened to fill the River Thames, which flowed along beside me on my walk back. It might not have cured me or got those years back, but at least I understood now. I could move on.

In lockdown, my day-to-day life has been very similar to that time I now look back on as awful, but with two key differences. This time, it's not voluntary, and I don't even have the little things, like football on the weekend, to keep me ticking over. I'm sitting here desperate to make up for lost time, to keep making progress on beating my issues, but instead I'm sat at home staring at four walls. It's all I can do not to lose my mind.

To be fair, though, my mental health during this latest lockdown period hasn't been quite as bad as I'd have expected it to be. A lot of my time at university felt a bit like New Year's Eve; there's so much pressure to have a good time that it can be hard to do exactly that. Since March last year, that pressure has been non-existent. Haven't been clubbing in a while? Neither has anyone else. Had a shit birthday? Well, it's certainly not down to a lack of friends this time. I've definitely missed my football, though, and it doesn't look like coming back anytime soon, either. As part of the route out of this lockdown, the government and Football Association, in all their wisdom, have allowed competitive football to return from April but without the presence of fans at any level. The FA Vase is set to continue, but behind closed doors. My chances of completing the 'road to Wembley' this year don't exactly look great.

It's not all bad news, though, and there's finally light at the end of the tunnel. It's April now, we've been under tough restrictions for nearly four months, but crucially there's a way out. In February, the government released a roadmap for easing the restrictions that have blunted so many people's lives over the last year or so. By mid-June, in theory, all limits on social contact will be removed. That will be it. We'll be free. What's more, the process of moving house to live with Tom and Dan, my close mates and fellow fans of shit football, has finally got off the ground. Indeed, over the three months in which there's been little else to do, we've sorted everything out. We move into a converted warehouse apartment in Aldgate the day after the FA Vase fourth-round ties are due to be played. The clouds of despair that have formed in my head over the last few months are starting to clear. I have a vision for the future, a way out, and it looks exciting.

Most normal people would spend their final day before moving house preparing for that move, maybe packing, maybe researching the local area, maybe just saying goodbye to friends and family. Instead, I've got a crackpot plan to attend a Vase tie despite the fact everything is behind closed doors. It's a plan that harks back to some of the happier times of my childhood, the rays of sunshine that beamed through the clouds of anxiety and depression.

In December 2012, as an enthusiastic and slightly odd 14-year-old student, I considered it a crying shame that many of the random football matches I went to were never recorded on video. Someone could score an unreal volley in off the crossbar from 35 yards and you would never be able to watch it back. Nobody ever did score an unreal volley from 35 yards, of course, but still, the thought was there. Along with an equally odd school-mate, I brought along a camera I found in the back of a cupboard to Walton & Hersham vs Corinthian-Casuals in the Ryman Division One South, and the rest, they say, is history. Well, not quite, but for five years my school-mate and I gradually developed a non-league highlights company that ended up being actually pretty good at what it did. We even had several job offers to take on filming roles elsewhere full time, but turned them down to ensure we had the weekends free to watch Sutton United.

There were some fantastic moments too, despite the 35-yard-volley-in-off-the-crossbar dream never quite coming to fruition. The name, Fox in the Box Productions, came after that fixture at Walton & Hersham was briefly halted by a probably quite confused fox running across the pitch. Over the following years, we travelled round a series of quaint and often crumbling non-league grounds, capturing moments of occasional genius and occasional comedy in a snapshot for ever. We didn't make much money, largely out of choice, but had the gratitude of players, coaches and fans alike to encourage us to keep coming back. We immortalised the day Egham Town won the league, and made it into a DVD; we covered a touring team from Argentina playing in Sutton; we travelled up to Sheffield with the London Bees team for a WSL Continental Cup quarter-final. Away from the matches themselves, one of my favourite memories is when we messed about filming a ridiculous 'farewell video' for Walton Casuals' condemned Waterside Stadium so we could spend the day having a kickabout on the pitch. Some of our most notable post-match interviewees included then-Leatherhead manager Jimmy Bullard and then-England assistant manager Ray Lewington, down at Molesey to watch his son Craig play. There were even a couple of times when we went viral in the national media, the first time coming after we captured the Kingstonian goalkeeper jumping into the terraces after a game to throw punches at the Bognor Regis supporters who had been giving him abuse all game (the second being when a goalkeeper scored against Sutton from a drop-kick in the last minute, of course). Perhaps the main thing Fox in the Box Productions achieved, though, was getting me out of the house at a time when I was often struggling mentally elsewhere. Those short, sharp bursts of joy helped get me through.

Sadly, it came to an end in 2017 as my mate and I both left for university, at which point the world of non-league football had adapted to have fairly widespread video coverage of its games anyway, a trend I like to think we played a part in. The camera was put away in storage and I thought that was it, my filming days were over. It would have probably stayed that way too, but one of the perks of being a cameraman was getting a press pass for the day. And, of course, a press pass is still valid even for games played without fans in attendance. Digging the camera back out of storage and looking around at the fixtures, it was clear that Sutton Common Rovers' tie at home to Barnet-based Hadley was my best bet for securing that golden ticket once more.

Rovers, whom I'd seen beat Southall 4-0 in the second round, were a club I'd covered plenty of times during my Fox in the Box days. They had actually been playing as Mole Valley SCR when I first filmed one of their games, an inauspicious 4-1 home defeat to Cove in the Combined Counties Premier Challenge Cup. A couple of years later, they ended their exile from Sutton by moving in at Gander Green Lane, home of Sutton United, of course, and my relationship with them got closer as they developed a close rapport with the side I support. With the club run by the exact same people as the last time I'd picked up a camera, I figured I had a pretty decent chance of being let in to cover their big FA Vase fourth-round tie. As it happened, I was right.

Initially, when I had set out to do this 'road to Wembley', the plan had been not to attend the same venue twice but, truly in this case, beggars can't be choosers. Besides, what better venue to attend twice than Gander Green Lane? To make my absence this season at 'the home of football' (as the plastic sheeting above the dilapidated park-side terrace describes it) particularly painful, Sutton United have found themselves in an unlikely title race. At one stage over lockdown, we got as far as six points clear at the top of the league, being made odds-on favourites with most bookmakers to win the league and secure promotion to League Two for the first time in our history. Don't get me wrong, it's been incredible to watch and helps me get through the days knowing we've got something special to play for at the weekends, but only being able to see it on a stream is painful. Visions of having to celebrate a historic achievement on a Zoom call plague me each time we get a good result. It seems to be more stressful watching at home as well; there's no outlet for my emotions. Whereas usually going to the football was my main form of catharsis, it has the opposite effect now. Managing to finally get to a game in the flesh after four long months of lockdown is a relief, even if it is one that is behind closed doors for everyone else.

It might not be a Sutton United fixture, but it still promises to be a lively match. The FA Vase has taken on extra meaning for the clubs involved since February, when the league season was unsurprisingly curtailed, given the repeated lockdowns preventing fixtures being played. All in all, Sutton Common had managed 13 league fixtures at this point, and their Vase opponents Hadley just eight. Understandably, nobody really fancied trying to fit 30-odd games into the remaining three months of the season. Lose the FA Vase tie today, though, and the season is over. Add to that incentive the fact that, with just 32 sides left in the competition, a place at the Wembley final due to be held in late May (with fans in attendance) is a very achievable prize.

Despite all the positives, playing behind closed doors isn't easy financially for clubs at this level. One of the remaining 32 clubs, Stowmarket Town, waved the white flag and dropped out of the competition, giving Cobham a bye to the last 16. The FA, to try and help matters, laughably offered each club playing behind closed doors a £100 payment. It's not even enough to pay the match officials. It's clear there are other issues to playing behind closed doors as I rock up at Gander Green Lane 20 minutes before kick-off – all the toilets in the ground are locked. Having necked a large bottle of Coke on the train, anticipating the sweet release of a piss in the park-side urinal upon arrival, I've been caught rather short. Now inside the ground, having gone through the Covid checks on entry, I'm trapped. With no route out again, I hope the match is a quick one.

The kick-off time is a slightly weird one, 4.15pm, owing to the funeral of Prince Philip at the typical non-league kick-off time of Saturday at three o'clock. The change has thrown me somewhat, my body clock still firmly acclimatised to the traditional schedule even though I've only been with it at all over the last few months via a live stream. Indeed, I actually woke up in the morning thinking it was a Sunday. It's hard to pick a favourite for this one as the sides warm up. Of their 13 league games played before the curtailment, Sutton Common managed 11 wins and two draws, being comfortably clear at the top when the axe fell. Hadley play in the Essex Senior League, despite not being based in Essex but, to paraphrase the comedian James Acaster, the searing doubts that this may have caused them haven't come to fruition, as they managed seven wins from eight games. Hadley's manager is clearly aware of how tight it will be, warning his team, 'No fucking about chatting to each other,' as they go into a passing drill for the final stage of the warm-up.

Despite the fixture being officially 'behind closed doors', a few gentlemen, who make no attempt to hide their allegiances to the away side, have made it in, and stand just along from where I've positioned the camera. Presumably they're directors or club officials of some sort, but aren't held back by any sense of duty or behavioural code as they throw themselves into the occasion, even singing the odd song in support of their side. One man has smuggled in a can of lager, turning away from the pitch to open it, giving a couple of shifty glances to each side before turning back round to watch the game. He misses a Sutton Common penalty shout in doing so, but still tells the home side's centre-forward to shut up as he continues his protestations to the referee. Lucky for the lager man, the referee agrees with him and nothing is given.

After ten minutes or so, I remember why I stopped bothering with the filming stuff. Looking down the viewfinder of the camera, you can't actually see anything. Hadley hit the bar after a scramble from a free kick, but I can't work out for the life of me what happens in the build-up. It doesn't take an eagle eye to spot that one of the visitors' main threats is their long throw, though. There are oohs and aahs of anticipation from the Hadley 'supporters' next to me every time Bradley Marriot hurls the ball towards the crowded Sutton Common penalty area. By and large, though, Sutton deal with it well and are the better side early on. They take the lead on 19 minutes as well, a brilliant finish from Kyle Henry, the star of the Southall fixture a couple of rounds back, after Hadley can't quite clear their lines. Still not overly impressed, the Sutton manager tells his players to 'liven up' as they walk back to the centre spot.

They don't liven up, though; far from it. Whereas before they had looked slick and smooth with their passing, making Hadley do the running, standards start to slip. The Barnet-based side come into it more, mostly through the quick feet of Solomon Ofori, who seems capable of gliding past defenders as if they aren't even there. It never quite comes off, though; a touch too many being taken as a good pass isn't on, and Sutton Common keep them just about at arm's length. The game falls into a lull, and my daydreaming spell is only broken when one of the Hadley contingent to my right bizarrely yells, 'That's not a booking, you insult the laws of the game,' at the ref, after perhaps the clearest booking you will ever see. Just as half-time looms, Hadley break forward and the striker (I can't tell who it is through the bloody viewfinder) is poleaxed by two defenders. Billy Baird steps up and crashes the penalty home to bring the sides level, the whistle for the break following seconds after the restart.

Though I moan about the view through the camera, really I'm just pleased to be there. I'm aware that I'm in a fraction of a percentage, an elite group, of people able to attend a football match today. On top of the release of just getting out of the house, I can feel that sense of purpose that drove me to set up Fox in the Box Productions in the first place. This is a massive event for both clubs, and without me there would be no permanent video record of their big day. A sense of purpose isn't exactly easy to find at a time when all you can do all day is sit inside and eat packets of crisps while watching four consecutive football matches on the TV, and so the end result probably means as much to me as it will for the players of the winning team.

Hadley start the second half a substitute down, after the long-haired one powers a wayward shot into one of the back gardens behind the terrace and has to climb the fence to get it back. Luckily, his services aren't required in the opening exchanges, and he soon reappears with a large grin on his face and the ball in his grasp. Having had something of a nomadic history themselves, Hadley, like Sutton Common, are probably just happy to have a venue to play at. A move to Brickfield Lane in 2016 finally bagged them a permanent venue with the requisite ground-grading for the level they'd progressed to, and followed spells playing at various other venues, including a less-developed incarnation of Brickfield Lane before having to leave in 2008. Perhaps the most interesting place they plied their trade was Chandoes Avenue in Whetstone, from 1978 to 1985. This might not sound like much on the face of it, but they shared the venue with the likes of Peter Shilton, Kevin Keegan and John Barnes, as it was also used as an England training base.

Unfortunately for Hadley, it seems as though they might have inherited their former stadium partners' inability to succeed in the big games as they give away a penalty early in the second period. There's some debate over the decision after the linesman appears to initially flag to indicate the ball had gone out of play before the penalty is awarded. Naturally, it's a debate I can't weigh in on very much with the view through the camera I have. The decision stands and Danny Fernandez steps up with the chance to put Sutton Common in front. His penalty is poor, though, more or less straight down the middle, and the keeper gets a hand to it. The ball loops up with a wicked spin that carries it back towards the goal, and the desperate keeper scrambles after it as Fernandez follows it in. It's the Hadley man who makes it first, but it looks like it's too late. The referee blows his whistle and points towards the centre-spot.

There's still confusion, though, and the Sutton Common players aren't quite sure what's been given. The ref says something and suddenly the Hadley players all rush to their now-triumphant goalkeeper, absolutely jubilant.

He's given a foul on the goalkeeper for the follow-up, not a goal. It's still 1-1. Minutes later, Sutton Common's talisman and goalscorer, Kyle Henry, limps off injured, and you begin to think it might not be their day.

As it happens, you would be absolutely right. The away side get their noses in front through a method that seems almost inevitable: the long throw. The keeper makes a hash of it, dropping the ball under little pressure for Shaz Anwar to fire home from inside the penalty box. Seemingly keen to avoid the scrutiny of his team-mates, he protests to the referee over a non-existent foul for just long enough for his defenders to leave him alone. Rather than bouncing back, Sutton Common struggle to create anything at all, their method of playing out from the back more akin to the Bell Inn than Barcelona. Eventually, Luke Alfano puts them out of their misery and makes it 3-1 with ten minutes to go. The Hadley contingent to my right aren't about to relax yet, though, as one demands a sin bin for a Sutton Common player, something which I'm not sure is even in the rules. Needless to say, he doesn't get it.

The 'sin bin' comment is about as exciting as the last ten minutes get as Hadley cruise through to the last 16. The full-time whistle is greeted with the Hadley lager man, who I'm fairly certain is still on the same can of lager nearly two hours later, dancing a little jig and declaring, 'That's the game, ladies and gentlemen.' It's been a strange atmosphere all day with barely 30 people in the ground, making it feel like a bit of a nothing game, like a pre-season friendly or even a Sunday morning match. On the pitch, though, it's a completely different story; both sides battling fiercely for every single ball, reflected in the vociferous celebrations

127

from the visiting players when the whistle goes. And who can blame them? It's another game of football to extend their season, another game closer to Wembley. They're almost within touching distance now, just three wins to go. The Wembley factor is clearly something weighing on the minds of those on the losing side too, as several slump to the floor in tears. Defender Aaron Goode in particular is inconsolable, having to be almost carried off the pitch by his manager. Goode has had a long and successful career predominantly at a higher level (even winning the Fox in the Box goal of the season competition for 2015/16) and has only recently dropped down to the level of the FA Vase. Now well into his 30s, he might not have many chances left to reach the famous arch.

Meanwhile, Sutton Common's goalkeeper takes out his frustrations in a way that rather unfortunately sums up the afternoon for him and his side. He belts the ball at the goal in anger but scuffs it wide, and has to go and surreptitiously retrieve it from the terrace behind the goal as the Hadley players continue to celebrate on the pitch. Luckily for him, the camera is off at this point as I look to scurry away to finally take my piss once aboard the first Thameslink train in any direction, preferably with a working toilet.

Though I'm not quite as disappointed as the boys in yellow, it wouldn't be completely unfair to describe this result as a bit of a pain in the arse for me. My plan for attending the following three rounds up until the Wembley final was to latch on to Sutton Common's own hypothetical run there. Now I'll have to find a new team to let me in: I hope Hadley are impressed with the footage I've come up with. Failing that, I might have to practise my tree-climbing skills as I look to complete the remaining rounds by watching over the fence.

Still, though, even if today's game is the last game I make it to, picking up the camera again has unquestionably been worth it. I spend the evening, the night before I move house, simply watching back some of the videos I produced all those years ago. Whether a dour 0-0 draw or a cup final thriller, they all bring back memories that put a broad smile on my face. However badly I was struggling mentally in the rest of my life, the hours I had my camera at the football were an escape for me, a time when I could show off my skills and enjoy myself at the same time. I thought I was just capturing the football in time, when really I was capturing my teenage happiness itself. Getting the camera out again has reignited that joy; it's brought a part of me back to life. If lockdown reminded me of the worst of my childhood, then the first game of football back has re-conjured the very best of it.

8

Hadley vs Binfield

24 April 2021

THE GAMES are coming thick and fast in the FA Vase, with each round up until the final on consecutive weekends, so I have just a week to find myself a game to attend in the last 16. The obvious choice would be Hadley, so on Monday morning I open up my laptop, navigate to the club website and call the number listed on the page. Picking up straight away, the guy on the other end is friendly, and we chat about their victory in the last round at Gander Green Lane as well as the general state of football amid the pandemic. I remark on how great it is to see my side, Sutton United, doing so well at least, and he concurs, which I find a bit strange. 'Oh, I've probably watched them as much as you have this season,' he explains, 'my brother is the manager.'

The manager in question, Matt Gray, is becoming something of a hero at Sutton United with the side's performances this season. A semi-professional club operating on a shoestring budget in a league full of big professional sides, the target each year is invariably survival.

We started this season well, but there weren't even whispers of a promotion battle, the mantra being to get to 50 points: the milestone whereby your National League status is usually safe for another year. But as time has progressed, we've kept ourselves stubbornly hanging on in the title race; in fact, we've actually led the way for spells. The fanbase has started to believe, upgrading our wildest dreams from a play-off spot to perhaps even the title, an astonishing outcome which would take the club to a place it has never been before in its history: the Football League. As I tell proud brother Steve over the phone, if Matt Gray does pull it off, they'll probably erect a statue of him in Sutton High Street.

To help put this season into context, you have to look into the club's past, even just in recent times. I drew up a Sutton United 'bucket list' in 2015 after a disappointing season that had seen us slump to 15th in Conference South. It was designed to be ambitious but at least slightly realistic, things we could achieve over the course of my lifetime but not in any rush. The first item was to get promoted to the Conference Premier (now the National League Premier), which we did the very next year. The second item was to see us play a Premier League club in the FA Cup, which we did in spectacular style against Arsenal in the last 16 of the FA Cup the year after. We haven't quite managed the third yet, which was to play at Wembley, probably in the FA Trophy Final, but if we don't win the league then the play-offs would put us in touching distance of that goal. Reaching the Football League wasn't on that list, as it simply wasn't a realistic aim. Even now, one point off the top of the National League with nine games to play, it feels a bit unnatural. Matt and his brother at Hadley, Steve, can probably barely imagine the joy this unprecedented promotion would give not only to me but the entire town.

Matt Gray's popularity goes beyond just his record in terms of results too. He took over in the summer of 2019, following on from club legend Paul Doswell, a man who had masterminded two promotions and that famous FA Cup run. To say it was a tough act to follow is an understatement. I remember Gray's first game in charge, a pre-season friendly against Chelsea's development squad, where I was collecting money for homeless charity St Basils. The goal was to get people to chuck in their loose change, the odd five or ten pence here and there, and the biggest single donation of the day prior to the match had been Gray's £5. Half an hour after the game had finished, Gray wandered over to where I was counting the money and asked how I'd got on. When I told him the figure, he smiled, put a further £20 note in the box and went back into the bar to talk to the rest of the fans. As far as first impressions go, it wasn't bad at all. Results weren't fantastic early on, but when times were tough, he would listen to fans' concerns rather than hide away. Sure enough, he turned it round before long, though I doubt anyone thought he would turn it around quite this much.

Making a random phone call and having the brother of an almost God-like figure for you pick up is certainly a strange one, but it does no harm in helping endear myself to Steve and Hadley Football Club. After a long and unexpected chat about all things Sutton United, both myself and my now-flat-mate Dan are confirmed on the list for the Vase tie against Binfield at the weekend. The wonderfully small world of football has come good for me again.

As well as being the day I sort out attendance for the next round of the FA Vase, Monday is also my first full day in the new flat. Given the majority of my social interaction over the last year or so has been with my cats, finally moving is an important first step on my long journey towards hopefully becoming a functional human being again. During my time living at home since March 2020 and the first lockdown, the simple art of conversation has become alien to me, and I dread to think what it will be like to try and flirt again. I mean, I was never exactly an expert in the first place, but now? My only hope is that people's standards have dropped equally since last March, from an already pretty low bar. My teenage years now long behind me, I can feel the early signs of ageing start to hit me. My hairline is retreating faster than the Allied forces at Dunkirk, while my knees and ankles feel like they've been shot at every time I do anything beyond mild exercise. Each hangover I get is worse than the last, and perhaps most tellingly, I'm beginning to find that I would not care if nightclubs never opened up again.

It's about time, then, that I get on with my life again, and we couldn't have picked a better location. A converted wool storage warehouse, where series two of *Dragons' Den* was filmed, our new place is right in the heart of the city in Aldgate. Finally being away from home, free from the claustrophobia of the living arrangements there, I can't hide my excitement as we approach our first Friday night out. There's a pub just down from the underground station with an outdoor area which extends on to a public garden, meaning you can buy bottles from the Sainsbury's opposite and act as though you're one of the big shots paying £6 for a pint. The peak of the drunken conversation that ensues covers the fact that if there was a Football League for beer gardens, the one we're at would not be able to enter, as the grass was artificial. Despite this, we somehow get talking to actual normal people outside of our group and even bag an invite to an otherwise all-French house party in June. Plenty of time to brush up on the language skills, I guess.

Unfortunately, and somewhat typically, not being constrained by pub closing times means we remain chatting to the random French people until gone 3am, with a big day at Hadley coming up just a few hours later. Tom, our third flat-mate up from Bournemouth, goes to bed rather smug, leaving Dan and I to regret our life decisions when morning swings around soon after. Being in the centre of London has its perks, as Hadley's Brickfield Lane is barely over an hour away on public transport, but it's still a journey we make horribly hungover and feeling somewhat sorry for ourselves. The highlight, or perhaps the lowlight, is Dan panicking and tapping his bank card on the Oyster card reader of the bus after thinking his Oyster card itself had been rejected. Long story short, it hadn't, and Dan paid for his fare twice. Even the old bloke in a wheelchair on his way to Barnet Hospital bursts out laughing at the moment of realisation and the pained look it puts on Dan's face. Just moments before boarding, my new flat-mate had complained of his brain 'not working' today. He certainly wasn't wrong.

The football headlines over the last week or so have been overwhelmingly negative, so it's nice to get away from all the bullshit at Hadley. News of the 'Big Six' joining a bunch of similarly arrogant and out-of-touch Spanish and Italian sides in a breakaway 'European Super League' breaks the day after the Sutton Common Rovers vs Hadley fixture. The 12 founder sides were to play each other every year, as there was to be no relegation, with the winner presumably being decided on who has the largest annual turnover at the end of the financial year. Real Madrid president Florentino Pérez even called for matches to be made shorter than 90 minutes, as young people aren't interested in football any more apparently. Of course, 74-year-old billionaires are always the best people to decide what the average young person does and doesn't like.

The move was met with widespread anger by supporters, of course, but many talked also of their shock at what was happening. I have to admit, that's something I didn't get. It's a bit like someone being surprised their dog has died when the poor thing has had cancer for the last few years. Some might say the top flight of English football has had 'cancer' since before I was born, the advent of the Premier League starting an interminable slide towards financial gain and away from the supporters. The writing has been on the wall for some time, suggestions that would make more money for the already richest clubs being proposed every year. Don't believe me? Cast your mind back to 'Project Big Picture', a proposal from Liverpool and Manchester United leaked just a few months before the Super League saga, with the plan to cut the Premier League down to 18 teams to ensure there was more free space in the calendar for lucrative European games. The additional sticking point with both of these proposals comes with the fact they've tried to shovel this pile of shit down our throats in the middle of a global pandemic, a time when more than ever the fans need to feel valued by their teams and the clubs outside the Premier League protected. But, of course, the 'Big Six' and their owners couldn't care less about either of these things; never have done and never will do.

The attempted money-grabbing proposals are such big news that it even filters through to the Babestation texts Dan has been receiving since his 'prank call' to the channel up in Coventry. They're always a great source of entertainment, but this week's edition really cracks me up, 'Freemsg: In the studio, producers just [sic] ESL footy, it's so boring! Please call me and talk sex!'

We might not have found out who would win in a fight between a bald eagle and a German Shepherd, but at least we eventually got this little gem. Funnily enough, since I started going to watch Sutton United every week, rather than Arsenal at the Emirates Stadium, I've come up with what I think is a pretty good analogy. The Premier League is a bit like watching pornography. It might display your wildest dreams, fulfil all your fantasies, but it's a one-way relationship. You watch through a screen. The people on the other side of that screen not only don't care about you, they also don't even know you exist. They do their job to make money, and nothing more. By contrast, supporting your local club is like having a girlfriend who might not be a supermodel, might have her imperfections, but you love her all the same. Most importantly, she loves you back. The relationship is two-way, and it's very much real. If I miss a game at Sutton, I have people texting me asking where I am, asking if I'm OK. When I stopped going to Arsenal, nobody cared; they simply passed my ticket to the next person on the waiting list and had done with it. After the game at Sutton, I go to the bar and drink with the players, as well as catching up with all my mates. I stand where I want and chat to whom I want, and a season ticket costs me about as much as two games at the Emirates. There really is no comparison.

As far as footballing 'girlfriends' go, Hadley seems a stunner as Dan and I get off the bus in the village of Arkley, where the ground is situated. It's clearly a well-off area with huge gated houses running alongside the country road that leads there, yet Arkley has lost none of its character. The main feature is a little white windmill, resplendent in the spring sunshine, that is situated only 100 metres or so behind one of the goals at Brickfield Lane. It makes for an unusual and particularly quaint backdrop, one that must be a photographer's dream. The ground itself is accessible down an old-fashioned private road opposite a pub car park, now pitched with gazebos to fit the current social distancing laws, making it something of an awkward one to find. Hidden behind thatched cottages and tall trees, it's the last place you would expect to see a football ground. When we do eventually work it out, we're warmly greeted and handed a 2020/21 season ticket as our pass for the day. I'm glad the club have managed to find some use for them, given it hasn't exactly been a season rife with spectator opportunity.

It's a big occasion for both of the two sides involved, with neither having reached this stage before. Indeed, before this year, Hadley had only managed to get as far as the second round. Binfield, like Hadley, were going well in their league before the season curtailment in February, and are obviously challenging opponents. They've got the most unimaginative club badge I've ever seen, though, just 'Binfield FC' written in a font that looks like it's been taken from Microsoft PowerPoint. The only slight creative touch is replacing the dot above the two letter i's with a star, perhaps representing the two Hellenic League Floodlit Cups or Reading & District League Division One titles they've won. It's anyone's guess as to how they'd mark a third piece of silverware in either competition. An ambitious club, they've made clear their intention to progress up the football pyramid in the future, though two of their three FA Vase wins this season have been via a penalty shoot-out.

'They've got five ringers in from the Conference South,' one of the Hadley directors says accusingly to the bloke sitting next to him as I set my camera up in the stand. I have no idea if there's any truth to this at all, but it's not an outlandish claim. With league football in National League South also suspended, a player at that semi-professional level could hypothetically register with a side like Binfield to get a few games and a chance of playing at Wembley to boot. Once the competition was over, they could easily move back to their bigger semi-professional club. It's another quirky caveat to consider in a competition already packed full of idiosyncrasies.

The game kicks off and I set my phone to give me goal updates from the games involving Sutton's title rivals, Stockport County and Torquay United. We play later ourselves, in the BT Sport live televised slot against Eastleigh, but we probably won't make it back to the flat in time to catch any of it. Secretly, I think I'm quite glad. We're at the point where the pressure is causing me serious stress. Within the first couple of minutes, it looks like Binfield's alleged National League South ringers might carry them through as some excellent football leads to a golden chance, a cross from the left finding striker Sean Moore all alone at the far post. As his team-mates go to celebrate, though, he somehow scoops the ball over the bar from no more than two yards out. 'That's your let-off, that doesn't happen again,' yells the Hadley assistant manager, but his side don't need telling.

Binfield don't go on to dominate at all, though; in fact, it's very even. The home side's main threat is the same man as in the Sutton Common game, Solomon Ofori, though this time he's playing further up the pitch. He's one of the most frustrating footballers I've ever seen, capable of moments of genius in beating players but often lacking the final ball to follow. A third of the way through the first half, he leaves his marker for toast, bearing down on goal but ultimately getting caught in two minds and trying to square the ball with a defender clearly blocking the route to the Hadley striker. Like the opportunity Binfield had right at the start, it's a great chance; not the sort of chance that comes around often in a big game like this.

It's not the sort of game where the referee or linesman have a lot to do, but a woman supporting Binfield makes sure she doesn't let them slack off as she loudly criticises every decision that goes against them. Beyond the level of the man shouting 'you insult the laws of the game' at Sutton Common, she comes out with some particularly bizarre claims and is corrected by the referee's assessor on several occasions. Unsurprisingly, though, she stays quiet when a Hadley goal is disallowed for a push by the striker as the ball came in. To be fair, there aren't exactly many complaints from a Hadley perspective, either. The first half ends with just one more clear chance, again for Ofori, the highlight otherwise being a Binfield player falling over as he goes to pick up the ball for a throw-in.

Elsewhere, the news is encouraging. Stockport are unsurprisingly ahead at Boreham Wood, but Torquay, our closest challengers, are a goal down at home to Notts County. As Dan mooches over with a fresh cup of coffee designed to reactivate his brain, it gets even better. The early minutes of the second half over in Devon have seen the away side double their lead. Could this really happen? Could we win the league? Dan and I exchange a little nod of celebration, but sadly the manager's brother Steve is completing one of the many errands he has been tasked with, and so I can't excitedly pass the score on to him as well. With any luck, I'll give the good news at full time instead.

Perhaps hearing the words from the visiting side's manager on keeping up performance levels throughout the game, the loud Binfield woman takes it a bit too literally and continues to berate the officials for every decision. At one point, she even argues with the now-clearly exhausted assessor about whether the 'sin bin' rule is in use in the FA Vase or not. When being told that it absolutely definitely is, she declares, 'Well, that's pathetic,' and looks pointedly in the other direction. I don't disagree with her, and quite what a player would need to do to get sin-binned I don't know. It's certainly more lenient than my Sunday league games, where any sort of swear word used when speaking to the ref lands you ten minutes on the sidelines.

The game at Hadley remains tense, both sides clearly having the avoidance of defeat in mind. Hadley perhaps edge it, Alex Teniola hitting the underside of the crossbar ten minutes into the second half. Ofori gets through on goal for the third time with an excellently timed run, but his finish is only as good as his other two attempts, much to the displeasure of the home fans. To spare him embarrassment, some of the spectators in the main stand appeal for a penalty despite the fact the recovering defender wasn't within arm's reach of Ofori when the shot was struck.

Much like the Sutton Common game, the atmosphere is strange, with the number of media people and club officials in the ground meaning the attendance probably isn't too far off what it would be for an average pre-coronavirus league match. Still, though, it's worlds away from what it would be if it wasn't for the pandemic. In the previous season's competition, I managed to get to a last-16 tie at Atherstone, close to where I attended university. Just weeks before Covid-19 shut the football world down, there was a baying crowd of nearly 1,000 people in, giving a noticeable extra edge to the game. It wasn't the best game of football I'd ever seen, but the atmosphere gave it life in itself. Though the guys and girls that have made it in today are clearly desperate for their side to win, it's just not the same as having a capacity crowd packed inside a tiny stadium. For me, it's one of the main appeals of this competition at the latter stages. This season, it's been replaced by a bloke watching the game perched high up a tree behind one of the goals.

As the tension continues to ramp up at Brickfield Lane, it does so elsewhere as well, with the LiveScore app telling me Torquay have got a goal back with 15 minutes to play. It means I'll be watching the updates on my phone almost as much as the Hadley match itself as the minutes tick down. Not long to go now. To try and break the deadlock, Hadley make a sub, the young Jordan Edwards coming on for Alex Teniola. Laughing and joking with his fellow substitutes about the new lime green Nike boots he's purchased for the occasion, Edwards is all smiles as he enters the pitch hoping to mark his name in the Hadley history books. Less than five minutes later, the home side's full-back dives with both feet into a challenge he has no chance of winning and is shown the red card straight away by the ref. One of Hadley's coaches is unimpressed with the decision, trying to show the replay from the live stream of the game to the fourth official, but he's having none of it. Now needing to rebalance the team, cruelly, it's Edwards who is taken off again. The look on his face is devastating, and though his management team apologise and explain the situation, you can't help but feel sorry for the poor lad.

Down to ten men, Hadley take a completely different approach, shutting up shop to try and force penalties. Unsurprisingly, Binfield pile on the pressure but don't really create any clear-cut chances despite playing virtually all of the remainder of the game in the Hadley half. The match kicked off slightly late and goes into considerable added time, and those backing the hosts are as desperate for the full-time whistle to go here as I am for it to go at Torquay. With the Berkshire side still pressing, I finally get a notification on my phone bringing news from Devon.

Rather than being the release of the full-time whistle, though, it tells of a Torquay equaliser in the ninth minute of added time. An absolute hammer blow, I can't help but curse loudly to the skies as Binfield lose the ball, earning me some funny looks from those I'm sharing the stand with. Just as I try to explain, the referee blows for full time at Brickfield Lane. My mind is elsewhere, but here we're going straight to a penalty shoot-out.

Still moaning to Dan about the lack of defensive steel from Notts County (who beat us earlier in the season, of course), I train the camera on the goal at the wooded area of the ground where the penalties are set to be taken. Binfield take first and set the pace, a low penalty into the corner that beats the keeper despite him going the right way. To the delight of the referee-baiting Binfield fan, their first three penalties are all excellent, in fact, though matched by Hadley until their third effort. Billy Baird hits it so far over the bar that it's not even a threat to the bloke sat high in the branches of the tree behind the goal. The ball keeps rising, travelling out of view while still on a steep upward trajectory, to the point where it's almost impressive. If it was a goal kick off the ground, it would probably be a threat to the opposing keeper. Sadly, all this counts for nothing in a penalty shoot-out, and Hadley are 3-2 down with two penalties each to go.

The next Binfield penalty is as proficient as the others, tucked perfectly away in the bottom-left corner. Hadley must score. Teddy Stacey, brought off the bench specifically to take a penalty, is the man tasked with doing so. I've never been a fan of this branch of thinking, believing the pressure lumped on the taker often overrides any technical advantages they might otherwise have. Stacey clearly disagrees and puts his penalty into the exact same spot as the Binfield one before, leaving the visiting side's centre-back Liam Ferdinand with the chance to win it. He goes for the same penalty again, slotted into the bottom left corner, but drags it miles wide. It's almost as bad as the one Hadley missed earlier. Ferdinand's opposite number steps up for Hadley and duly sends it to sudden death.

Liam Gavin rolls the first sudden death spot-kick down the middle and into the back of the net for Binfield, leaving Solomon Ofori with the unenviable task of needing to score. You get the feeling that he's the last person you want on the job. Undoubtedly an exceptionally talented player, his game is plagued by the drawbacks of lacking final product and a tendency to crumble under pressure. It's not the ideal CV for this particular task. Ofori looks nervous right from the walk up to the spot, and sure enough his kick is weak and at the perfect height for Binfield keeper Chris Grace to save and make himself the hero. As the away side rush to celebrate and Ofori walks off disconsolate, Dan and I pack up to race home in the hope of catching the second half of the Sutton United game.

As it happens, we end up wishing we hadn't bothered. Eastleigh go 1-0 up as we're still on the tube, a goal right on half-time which is a good yard or two offside. Scrambling through the door with 20 minutes to go, we manage to get the stream set up but would have missed absolutely nothing if we hadn't. Without testing the keeper once, we slump to a 1-0 defeat that makes the positivity of half-time in the earlier game look a long way away indeed. Though our fate is still in our hands, it's Torquay who have the momentum in the run-in, and there's now no margin for error. The final eight games promise to raise my heart rate to the max as we look to achieve a piece of history that will be felt not only in Sutton but over in Hadley as well.

9

US Portsmouth vs Flackwell Heath

1 May 2021

FOR ALL the hustle and bustle of its millions of residents, London isn't half a lonely place at times. The late-night chat with our French neighbours last week, though hardly a buzzing party event, set sadly unrealistic expectations for my supposedly newfound social life up in Aldgate. Since then, I've been out only to go to the nearby Sainsbury's, and even there you're only interacting with a self-service machine. I'm so out of the loop I couldn't even manage that properly, not clocking the difference between the area where you put your goods after you've scanned them and the side bit where you move your recently purchased items to. It's all just the 'bagging area' to me, a concept I haven't had to get my head around in my time living 15 miles further south. The store assistant adding to my embarrassment by having to explain how to use the machine ends up being my only human interaction all week.

To break the monotony of it all, Dan and I go back on the FA Vase trail on Saturday, a full seven days after the

146

previous round, which itself was seven days after the round before that. Such a packed cup schedule would usually be unheard of, but I doubt anyone is complaining this year. It's not like there's anything else to do.

We're in a weird place with restrictions easing at the moment, a sort of nether zone where we're not technically in lockdown any more but not really *out* of it, either. One of the many ridiculous and frustrating rules is that fans still aren't allowed to attend FA Vase fixtures. The clubs involved rarely have more than 300 regular supporters, all of whom could safely attend with more than adequate social distancing still in place, but the government still will not budge. Even worse, the postponed 2019/20 FA Vase Final is due to take place at Wembley on the bank holiday Monday of this weekend, but fans aren't even allowed at that. There are 90,000 seats at Wembley, but not a single person supporting the finalists Hebburn or Consett Town can be allowed in. Given the League Cup Final between Manchester City and Tottenham a week earlier was played in front of 8,000 fans, the loyal backers of Hebburn and Consett hoping for a once-in-a-lifetime opportunity to see their side play at Wembley can feel particularly aggrieved.

My own 'road to Wembley' in the Vase this season isn't going to be made easy by the restrictions, either, with my filming contacts now exhausted. Rejections by all four home sides in the quarter-final mean Dan and I spend the week trying to work out at which ground it would be easiest to watch the game over the fence. Countless hours meticulously scouring Google Maps help identify either Leighton Town or United Services Portsmouth as our main targets, and at 10pm the day before the game we finally settle on the latter option. Tickets booked at the 11th hour, we get ready for a trip down to the south coast to try and catch a glimpse of a cup tie involving two sides we know nothing about and care nothing for.

'Why the hell are you doing that?' I hear you ask, and it's not an unreasonable question. 'Because I'm a sad bastard' wouldn't be an unreasonable answer, either, but there is more to it than just that, I suppose. With the world and most other elements of my life in stasis, the journey started out as something to look forward to at the weekend. With the 'rule of six' the mantra at the time, a game with 300 people present was essentially a major networking event, both with close friends and random people I'd never previously met. Since the end of the torturous lockdown that began in January, completing what is left of the road to Wembley has become a challenge, something to aim for. The sheer absurdity of travelling down to Portsmouth on a Saturday afternoon to try and watch over the fence has somehow made it even more entertaining. I will complete this mission, and not even simple common sense or any sort of introspection will stop me.

Dan is the fresher of the two of us as we make the trip down south, owing to his disappointing no-show at drinks the night before. With London still eerily quiet, I had decided to make the trip back to Sutton for the popular 'car park cans' at Sutton United's Gander Green Lane, even bringing Bournemouth-supporting flat-mate Tom along. Despite only having the slightest of colds, Dan declared himself unfit to join us, his rationale being that such an 'injury' on *Football Manager* warrants one to two days out of action. My argument that this is only an orange indicator, and not a red one (a recommendation of rest rather than being officially ruled out for those not versed in the best football game on the market), falls on deaf ears, and the poor soldier is tucked up in bed long before discussions over Sutton's title chances have concluded. An unconvincing 1-0 win at home to bottom side Barnet on Tuesday night has put us back on track, though the result was soured somewhat by Torquay nicking a stoppage-time winner in their own game to keep them top. With the Gulls very much the form side at the minute, there's no room for error as we chase history. Again, I'm grateful for the alternative entertainment of the FA Vase to take my mind off it for a bit. It's big pressure.

United Services Portsmouth, or US Portsmouth for short, play at the Royal Navy sports centre just minutes from Portsmouth Harbour. Named after one of the iconic British fleet that saw off the Spanish and French at the Battle of Trafalgar, HMS *Temeraire*, the football pitch is just a small part of an impressive facility. Free access is granted to all members of the services, with the general public also able to book in to play anything from basketball to badminton. The football stadium is situated within the complex, meaning the entrance is a good five-minute walk from any sight of the pitch, but given we're not allowed in today, that's not something we have to worry about. In fact, it's the slightly odd layout that means we have any chance of watching the game at all. Our Google Maps reconnaissance tells us that the fence separating the athletics ground (which hosts the football pitch) from the road is comprised of just a few railings, which you can easily see through. Though we'd have to stand on the pavement by the B2154, admittedly a fair way back from the pitch, our view otherwise will be perfectly clear. It's easy, this behind-closed-doors business.

It's pissing down with rain as the train pulls into Portsmouth Harbour, meaning we join a large number of other passengers in waiting it out on the platform, hoping more than expecting that the weather will soon turn. The station extends into the harbour itself, giving good views of the sea, which neither Dan nor myself have seen since the trip down to Bournemouth many months ago. My companion for the day can't believe it's been that long, desperately checking his Google Maps tracking history to try and jog his memory. The results of the search are predictably depressing: there was one week in which Dan didn't even leave his house, never mind travel outside of south London. You really have had to go out of your way just to escape over the last year or so.

There's a couple of hours to kill before the game starts, allowing us time to explore the city a bit. The HMS *Temeraire* sports complex is remarkably central, resisting the developments that so often take over any green space in a city centre these days. Dwarfed by several huge blocks of flats, it stands defiant as a symbol of the importance of the navy throughout the history of the area. A ten-minute stroll south takes you away from the hustle and bustle to Southsea Common, a large expanse of open space with a wonderful view across the entrance to the harbour. With global travel still effectively mothballed, there are very few ships to spot today. Despite the persistent rainfall, we sit there for a while on the grass, silent, just taking in the fact we're somewhere new. The reflective and somewhat sombre mood is only broken when Dan slips down a grass bank as he goes to get a closer view of the sea, putting smiles on the faces of two young children walking by as well as causing me to almost fall over myself with laughter.

As we head back towards the ground with kick-off approaching, rows of rundown student houses gradually give way to more upmarket properties once more, and eventually the stadium's main stand rises from it all. A brutalist solid concrete structure, it takes up less than half of one side of the touchline but probably houses around three-quarters of the total capacity of the football ground. Just past where it ends, the concrete gives way to the see-through fence that means we can watch the game today. As for the official entrance to go inside the stadium, well, it's practically in the next town. Even if we were invited in at this point, we'd probably miss the first ten minutes just walking round to get there.

It's just as well then that the plan of watching through the fence works out perfectly, the pitch just as visible as it appeared online. Sitting in a bus stop before kick-off to shelter from the relentless rainfall, we're passed by two US Portsmouth players, fully clad in their team tracksuit, carrying large crates of booze towards the ground. Clearly, they're hoping for, or perhaps expecting, a cup shock today. The home side are the last remaining side from the tenth tier in the competition, and have been for some time now. They've needed shock after shock after shock to get to the quarter-final, and are in no mood to stop now. Most of the sides from the lower rung that succeed in the FA Vase are dominant in their league, and though US Portsmouth didn't exactly do badly, they were comfortably behind both Laverstock & Ford and Alton Town when the season was curtailed. For them to get to Wembley would be absolutely incredible, make no mistake.

Their opponents today, Flackwell Heath, finished top of their ninth-tier league, the Hellenic League Premier Division. That said, they only managed seven league games before the curtailment, finishing a point ahead of fellow FA Vase quarter-finalists Binfield. They had actually won the league back in 2015 and were set for promotion to Division One Central of the Southern League, but the demotion of Clevedon Town due to issues with their floodlights meant Heath were to be switched instead to the Division One South and West, a move which would have resulted in significantly more travelling. The club declined promotion as a result, and have remained in England's ninth tier since. US Portsmouth have their own recent promotion horror story, having been top of the table at the time the coronavirus pandemic hit the UK. However, the league was ultimately rendered null and void, and promotion dreams were crushed as a result.

Perhaps unsurprisingly, Dan and I aren't the only ones with the bright idea of watching through the fence, as a rag-tag group of spectators begins to assemble. One elderly gentleman complains about not being allowed in, and I can't disagree with him. A large athletics venue, the stadium could easily hold 300 people while maintaining social distancing. Not even 200 metres away, Gunwharf Quays shopping centre is jam-packed, with few people making any effort to stay apart from each other. It's a crying shame, not only for the supporters but also the players, who have to play one of the biggest games of their lives in front of a smattering of club officials and members of the media.

There's never a bad year to do well in a cup competition, but for everyone involved it's undoubtedly the worst time for it. I wonder how much that will play on their minds over years to come, how great those feelings of 'what might have been' will be. Many won't get another chance.

The elderly man starts talking to us about his own personal connection to the home side – he used to play for the army football team at the venue in the 1960s. US Portsmouth themselves were only formed in 1962 as 'Portsmouth Royal Navy' and allowed only members of the armed forces to play for them until 2004. This change in policy came with the club being re-elected to the Wessex League, having previously been relegated in 2002, and sparked an immediate improvement in fortunes. Despite this, they haven't yet managed promotion out of Division One of the Wessex League, and the elderly bloke we're talking to reckons the navy team were always hopeless in the 1960s as well. Happy to let his rivalries from 60 years ago slide, though, he does seem to be supporting the home side today.

US Portsmouth certainly don't seem hopeless today, though Flackwell Heath are the better side in the opening stages. They look to play a neat passing game, with everyone comfortable on the ball, and apply all the early pressure. They're hampered somewhat, however, by the pitch, which resembles a car park full of little potholes. The rain that's currently falling is the first the region has had in what seems like months, and the pitch has been baked into submission by the summer sun. It suits the hosts down to the ground, though, with their attacking coming predominantly on the counter with precise balls over the top. It would be unfair to describe it as mere 'long-ball football', as they appear to work out their opponent's weakness and play to it early on. Dressed in the red and blue stripes of Crystal Palace, they share the pragmatism of the underdog so often associated with the south London side. Another one of the rabble watching beside me through the fence is impressed. A local man of Indian origin, he only popped out of his flat to get bread and milk but half an hour later is still stood transfixed, not taking his eyes away from the game. He asks me about the significance of the fixture, and seems drawn in by the prospect of a Wembley final for his local side. Impressively, he lasts until almost half-time before receiving a call from his angry significant other, questioning why his grocery run is taking quite so long. Rather than the embarrassment of admitting that he's watching an amateur football match through a fence, the man instead informs her that he's cheating on her as he rushes back towards the flat. Well, not really, but it's probably not a bad idea.

The man gets to see a goal before he leaves, though, and it's a goal for the home side too. Predictably, it comes from a cross-field diagonal ball, exposing Flackwell Heath's Achilles' heel. Striker James Franklyn gets between two defenders and sends a delicate lob over the keeper's head, sending the elderly gentleman, the Indian man and a middle-aged couple clad in red and blue scarves wild. Presumably, those in the stadium are pretty happy about it too, but with us so far back from the pitch it's hard to tell. The main stand, built with 500 seats but with very few in use today, sits alongside our vantage point and so the noise emanating from it is directed away from us. We can barely even hear the shouts of the players. It's got all the atmosphere of watching on the TV but the view of a crap non-league away end. Still, football is football, and there's a story on our hands if US Portsmouth can hang on.

With it so hard to get into the atmosphere of the game, I find myself people-watching as my mind drifts. The highlight is when two young women dressed for a day out at Gunwharf Quays walk past, and one asks the other if she knows what the event taking place on the football pitch is. 'Of course,' she says, 'it's the army versus navy game.' The confidence with which she makes this fact up wins her friend over, and none of the rabble have the heart to correct her. Back on the pitch, Flackwell Heath miss a golden opportunity for an equaliser after the Portsmouth keeper drops the ball in a scramble. If only he had the confidence of the woman walking past, the error would have been easily avoided. Mind you, it's hard to tell whether it was really an error at all, given one of the stewards inside the ground has stood right across my line of view for the far goal. If there's any further scoring, I need it up the near side if I want to see it. Portsmouth do hit the bar, which the elderly gentleman is very quick to point out was from their first corner of the game, but the half-time whistle goes not long after, with the score still 1-0 to the hosts.

Meanwhile, Sutton United lead Aldershot 2-1 at half-time as we look to keep our unlikely title dreams on track. As I tell Dan the score, the elderly gentleman's eyes light up.

'Is that Sutton United you're talking about? The one in south London?'

It turns out that the army weren't the only side this bloke played for back in the day. For most of the break, he regales us with tales of his days at the club I love so much in the early 1960s, nearly 40 years before I was born. It appears very little changed at Gander Green Lane until very recently, as he complains about the state of the pitch, which slowed him down as an otherwise tricky right-winger. The pitch had stayed very much 'dogshit', in his own words, until the artificial surface was installed in the summer of 2015. Should we pull off the unthinkable and win promotion to the Football League, it will no doubt be dogshit again, as we would need to pull the artificial pitch up and replace it with grass. The underground stream that flows beneath the pitch means that before long the grass is replaced by sand. The elderly gentleman seems grateful for the explanation, and describes games on a particularly heavy pitch as being like a game of golf. The art for the left-back is to loft the ball into the sand patch (the bunker), where it will hold up for the winger to run on to. Of course, this is considered preferable in the Football League to a free-flowing game played on a laser-flat artificial pitch. You might expect someone in their 80s to be a bit of a traditionalist, but the elderly gentleman sees the Football League's pitch policy as 'a load of bollocks'.

We chat for almost the entirety of the break, only briefly interrupted by Dan spilling his milkshake all over the two of us. In a true 'brain-not-working' moment, he'd gone to shake the drink as instructed by the words on the side of the bottle, only to forget he'd already taken the lid off. He's not the only one embarrassing themselves at the break, though. With the traffic on the B-road behind us more or less static, a woman waiting in her car leans out and asks the score. One lad, who has been coming and going somewhat with his mate, informs her the game is goalless.

When everyone else there explains that it is in fact 1-0, his jaw drops. It turns out the two of them have travelled up from Flackwell Heath but attempted the long trek round to the other side of the sports complex to see if they could get inside the ground. During this time, they missed the only goal of the game so far and didn't realise until now. Having been chatting away before, the two of them go silent, though the woman in the car at least is happy.

There are more new spectators for the second half, as the place of the Indian man is taken by a teenager who informs us his cousin is the US Portsmouth left-back. Having just got away from work, he's as frustrated as anyone else not to be inside the ground. The experience is clearly just as nervy for him from behind the fence, though, as the visiting side start to push forward even more. A through ball picks out former Reading youngster Khalid Simmo, who is in on goal. He successfully chips the keeper and the ball rolls towards the line, but it lacks any real pace and the Portsmouth defenders are able to recover and clear. Winger Simmo continues to act as Flackwell Heath's main threat, with the elderly gentleman particularly impressed with the man playing in his former position. Just minutes after the failed attempt at chipping the keeper, he beats his man out wide and gets into a dangerous position to whip a cross in. Unfortunately for him, the ball ends up in the sandpit for the long jump rather than the back of the net. Time, I'm sure, moves slowly for the US Portsmouth faithful as their visitors continue to ramp up the pressure.

Other than the time they launch a quick free kick into the arse of one of their own players, the home side seem fairly adept at game management, though. Possession predominantly goes the way of the Berkshire side, but US Portsmouth don't seem to care. Their shape is good, making it hard for Flackwell Heath to play through the lines, and whenever the ball goes long, the two bald centre-backs win every single header. Their aura is almost threatening, and the opposing centre-forwards generally don't even bother challenging them. 'Imagine if we got to Wembley, just imagine,' repeats the left-back's cousin stood next to me as he seems to be shaking with nerves. They reach the last ten minutes still a goal up, but even then the pressure is immense. Corner after corner is launched into the box, but nothing comes of any of them. You can taste Flackwell Heath's frustration with just minutes left to salvage their Wembley dream.

US Portsmouth remain a threat on the counter, though, and break forward with three minutes to go. I can't really see what's happening, as the ball is up the far end and the steward still hasn't moved, but the ball suddenly floats across into the penalty box where Harry Sargeant is waiting unmarked. From our vantage point, his header seems to creep towards goal, barely moving, but still ends up inside the post with the keeper beaten. The players go ballistic at the goal, which surely now books their place in the FA Vase semi-final. They're one game from Wembley.

In our pavement viewing area, there is an entire rainbow of different reactions to the goal. The left-back's cousin is beside himself with joy, jumping up and down and muttering about Wembley under his breath. The elderly former Sutton player looks pleased but more reserved, not overly concerned with the events unfolding in front of him. By contrast, the two Flackwell Heath fans somehow look even more depressed than when they discovered it wasn't 0-0 at half-time, and one of the club officials lucky enough to have made it inside the ground walks over to share his grievances with them through the fence. Dan and I step back and take in the absurdity of the situation. It should have been greeted with loud roars heard for miles around. Instead, you could say it's been witnessed almost literally by one man and his dog, as someone walks a white Labrador just behind where those watching through the fence are gathered.

It's not technically over for Flackwell Heath, not yet anyway, but their race looks run. Having put so much pressure on without scoring, you don't feel as though their fortunes are going to change so dramatically now. They manage to sum up their day quite well when Mitchell Parker hangs a cross towards the far post, the ball travelling over everyone, including the goalkeeper, and hitting the top of the crossbar. It comes back into play off the woodwork, but the home side react first to get the ball away. Seconds later, the full-time whistle goes and celebrations just as loud as for the second goal erupt, only this time more prolonged. Remarkably, it's the sixth time in this competition that US Portsmouth have knocked out a team from the division above them. The chants of 'Wemberley' among the jubilant players tell you all you need to know. Repeat their trick one more time and they'll be playing under the famous arch in less than a month's time.

As the two Flackwell Heath supporters watching with us skulk off, the elderly gentleman gets confused and apologises to Dan and I for his over-exuberant celebrations. By the time he realises we're not the two away fans in the crowd of around ten, the actual 'victims' are long gone. Quite as to why he's apologising anyway, I don't know. Right next to him, the other home supporters are much more vociferous in their revelries, but even that is nothing compared to what is going on across the fence and on the pitch. The singing is still in full flow as we head back towards the train station, with those beers the substitutes acquired before the game looking like a good investment now. I'm not in a bad mood myself, either – the full-time whistle has gone over at Sutton United, and there's news of a 3-1 win for the amber and chocolates. With six games to go, we're still just about in the driving seat. With any luck, we'll soon add another smile to not only my face but also that of the elderly gentleman who played his part for the club all those years ago.

10

Warrington Rylands vs Walsall Wood

15 May 2021

US PORTSMOUTH'S fairytale story never did come off. Up against Binfield in the semi-final, the vanquishers of Hadley in the round of 16, the underdogs led until the last ten minutes, when Liam Ferdinand finally equalised to send the game to penalties. Ferdinand was presumably one of the 'Conference South ringers' described by the angry Hadley supporter a few weeks back, having signed halfway through the season from Harrow Borough, who play two divisions above Binfield in the Southern League Premier South. The penalty specialists then pulled it off from 12 yards again, keeper Chris Grace the hero, as he had been at Hadley. To make matters even more devastating for Portsmouth, they had led the shoot-out after three penalties each, and the first one they missed was from Cameron Quirke, who was brought on specifically to take a spot-kick. To be fair to Binfield, describing them as mere 'penalty specialists' is perhaps a bit harsh given they'd hammered Long Eaton 5-0 in the quarter-final. They'll be a tough opponent for the winner of the other semi-final, in which Warrington Rylands take on Walsall Wood.

That semi-final is taking place today, a week after US Portsmouth's tie, for scheduling reasons that could only have come to pass in this mad pandemic-afflicted year. Warrington Rylands were due to face Hebburn Town in the quarter-final on Saturday, 1 May, the same day the other three fixtures were settled, including US Portsmouth's win over Flackwell Heath. However, the final of the 2019/20 edition of the FA Vase was scheduled for bank holiday Monday, 3 May – and Hebburn were in it. To allow the Tyneside club some rest before their big day, the 2020/21 quarter-final against Warrington Rylands was pushed back a week, making it the same day as the other semi-final. Confused? Me too.

With fans not allowed into last season's final, I sat at home and watched the big game on my laptop, wishing like thousands of others that I could be there. From start to finish, it was an incredible match. Pre-match headlines had centred around the fact that identical twin brothers Arjun and Amar Purewal were both playing in the fixture, and for opposing sides too. The pair, who co-own a sports coaching company, spoke prior to the game about looking to break down barriers as they became the first British South Asians to face each other at Wembley Stadium. Now 31 years old, Arjun and Amar have experience in making history dating 13 years back, as they became the first twins ever to score in the same FA Cup tie back in 2008. Then playing for the same side, Bishop Auckland (in a 3-2 win against Darlington RA), the positions they play in mean that facing each other carried particular interest before the game. Amar, of Hebburn, is a centre-forward, while Arjun plays at centre-back for Consett. He was tasked with marking his twin brother on the big stage.

Having dominated the Northern League for the last couple of years, including netting double figures on several occasions, Hebburn were undoubtedly the favourites, but it was Consett who took the lead when Saudi Arabian Northumbria University student Ali Alshabeeb rounded the keeper to slot home. The lead lasted for all of a minute, and who would score the equaliser but Amar Purewal? Put through by an incisive pass virtually straight from kick-off, he kept his calm to slot home just before brother Arjun got across to tackle him. Consett led again in the 41st minute through a Dale Pearson goal, but still found themselves going into the break level as Hebburn hit back immediately once more, former Newcastle United man Michael Richardson the scorer. Richardson, a midfielder, had averaged better than a goal every two games for Hebburn since joining the club in 2018, and already had an FA Vase winners' medal to his name when he played his part in a 4-0 final win over Cleethorpes Town with South Shields in 2017.

With the first half having been so entertaining, it was probably natural for the second period to be something of an anti-climax. Still, my flat-mates Dan and Tom watched on engrossed throughout, admitting they wouldn't have expected to see such a high-quality game between two ninth-tier sides. Both spoke of their desire to attend the FA Vase Final in years to come, and with tickets usually priced around £20, how could they not? Despite the lull in the pace of the game, there was still more drama to follow as

Hebburn nicked a late winner to lift the famous trophy for the first time. The following week, they were knocked out of the FA Vase's 2020/21 edition, losing 1-0 to Warrington Rylands, meaning their defence of the trophy lasted a full five days. I feel like that has to be some sort of record.

The unique fixture schedule of this season means the semi-final is just seven days later and, of course, I'm heading up to Merseyside for the final game on my FA Vase trail before the big Wembley finale. With family business to attend on final day, Dan is keen to make it up to Warrington with me, but ticket prices for the train journey could prove a stumbling block. To try and get around it, we use some 'ticket-splitting' site, a magical gizmo that saves you nearly half of the original price. The caveat is that it puts you into a game of musical chairs between stations, with a different booking for each leg of the journey, but it doesn't seem to be a problem on this particular journey. Unsurprisingly, people aren't exactly queuing up for the early morning London Euston to Liverpool Lime Street service during the middle of a pandemic. Along with us on the journey is a stepladder we picked up from a local community Facebook group, our secret weapon in our hope of watching the game. Behind closed doors again, we've carried out the now-usual Google Maps scouting mission to see if watching over the fence is viable. It looks like it might well be – but the images online are from more than ten years ago. We could well be in for a nasty surprise.

Warrington Rylands 1906 Football Club, to give them their full name, have come a hell of a long way in the last ten years. They were initially founded back in, no prizes for guessing this one, 1906 as a works team for the local wire manufacturer, and have spent the vast majority of their history playing in various local leagues. Little did they know it at the time, but their path in history was to be changed forever in the 1970s, when a local man by the name of Paul Stretford turned out for the club. In 1987, Stretford founded Proactive Sports Management, which went on to represent several top-level professional footballers, most notably Wayne Rooney. Starting out at a time when football agents were just beginning to make big money, the former Rylands player was one of the biggest in the business and amassed a significant fortune from his role. Keen to leave a legacy, Stretford started investing in Rylands from the 2012/13 season, with a full takeover completed six years later. Since then, Rylands have won two consecutive promotions to reach the ninth tier of English football, where they now play in the North West Counties Football League Premier Division. Across the last couple of Covid-hit seasons, they've challenged firmly at the top of it.

On top of all of the on-pitch successes Warrington Rylands and Paul Stretford have seen recently, there has also been £100,000 of ground improvements since 2016. A significant sum of money at this level, it means there's a good chance we won't even be able to watch over the fence, having travelled 200 miles to do so. Perhaps if Albert Einstein were still alive he would like to update his definition of insanity based on our journey today. To add to the sense of trepidation, Dan and I are met by torrential rain as we head outside at Warrington Bank Quay station. Getting plenty of funny looks as we trudge down the road without any sort of waterproofs and carrying a large stepladder, we're desperate to find shelter anywhere possible, so you can imagine the sense of relief when like an oasis in the barren desert, a Wetherspoons pub with covered outdoor seating appears on the horizon. Water streaming off the flimsy-looking gazebos pitched outside on the street, we dive for cover as the howling wind peppers raindrops at us with stinging ferocity.

Now in mid-May, we're just two days away from the next planned easing of restrictions. From Monday, people can drink inside pubs, but for now we can only gaze longingly at the promised land of stained carpets and wonky tables. Every time we need the toilet we have to walk through it to get there, and the warmth means it's a trip to treasure as we look to briefly defrost before moving back to the pissing rain for the rest of our stay. The outdoor area is small but predictably still far from full as only hardcore pub drinkers brave the inclement weather to sip on their morning pints. In fact, Dan and I make up half the entire clientele. One of the other two blokes there is a stereotypical ale drinker, tucked away in the corner with a flat cap, completing the crossword in the morning paper. He's on first-name terms with the staff working there today, and is clearly far too hardened and committed to be put off by a bit of rain. The other, a long-haired middle-aged man in an England shirt drinking a pint of lager, gets talking to us.

It turns out this long-haired man is a local groundhopper and, in a similarly desperate state to me after the suspension of local football for most of this year, has plans to attend a Cheshire League fixture this afternoon. These plans are soon scrapped when we tell him of our destination this afternoon, seemingly doing a good job of selling the merits of the FA Vase. We swap stories from the various random football matches we've seen, though my tales of Tuesday night away days at Barrow aren't a patch on some of his highlights. From entering a free competition, he wangled an all-expenses-paid trip to South Africa for the 2010 World Cup, the only downside being he had to put up with watching England's dour performances in all four games they played. Another free competition win saw him fly out to Marseille for Euro 2016, where he watched a game sat alongside former professional footballer and now leading pundit Alex Scott. As he elaborates on both of these tales, I make a mental note to enter some free competitions myself.

A couple of hours later, having recounted these stories alongside many more, the long-haired man excuses himself and sets off on a slightly less exciting trip: to Warrington Asda before the game. He leaves with such a stark warning about the local buses that Dan and I decide to walk the mile and a half to the ground instead. Given we're still lugging around a significantly sized stepladder between us, this arguably isn't the greatest idea, but we still make it to Gorsey Lane in good time for kick-off. Thankfully, the £100,000 of ground improvements have done nothing to stop chancers with a stepladder from watching the game over the fence; we set our little viewing platform up in line with the edge of the penalty box at one end. Nobody inside Gorsey Lane seems too bothered at us being there; indeed, one club official comes round and thanks us for making the effort, saying he wishes he could let us in. The two police officers inside the ground, clearly happy just to be there themselves, do nothing to move us on.

Like the train station we arrived at, which lies in the shadow of a giant Unilever manufacturing plant, the suburb in which the ground is situated perfectly fits the stereotype of 'Industrial North'. A row of old terraced houses runs behind the side where we pitch our stepladder, with a local railway line passing high above the goal to our right-hand side. At the foot of it lies a small caravan site, and as you walk towards it, graffiti on the breeze-block concrete wall by the overgrown garden of the funeral centre reads 'Tracy Williams is a grass'. The wonder of Google Maps' image history tells you that nobody has bothered to remove that graffiti in ten long years. A modern low-rise block of flats behind the other goal completes the local housing estate, which the football ground is tucked on the edge of. Just the other side of it is the first green space Dan and I have come across on our half-an-hour-or-so trek from the town centre.

Our view of the match is good, far better than at US Portsmouth two weeks ago. The pitch is tightly pressed up against the standing area inside the ground, which in turn is only a couple of metres from the perimeter fence which we're standing behind, meaning our viewpoint is like being inside the ground itself. The music blaring out from the PA system has clearly been carefully selected, as the Clash's 'London Calling' reminds both sides what's at stake, before David Bowie's iconic voice implores the home side to make themselves heroes, just for one day. Presumably, they'd quite like to be heroes for another day too, if they did make it to the Wembley final, though sadly I don't think Bowie had this exact situation in mind when he came to write his story of two lovers separated by the Berlin Wall.

With Rylands' link to the big time through owner Paul Stretford, they have had plenty of support on social media in the week leading up to the game from big names such as Harry Maguire and Gary Neville. Wayne Rooney even popped down to the Tuesday night training session to talk to the players about dealing with big occasions, just three days after his Derby County side secured Championship survival with a 79th-minute goal on the final day of the season. Everton tweeted their support on the morning of the game too, with Rylands' assistant manager Fraser Ablett's late father, Gary, the only man to have won the FA Cup with both Liverpool and Everton. Ablett Senior had been growing into his coaching career with a role assisting Roy Keane at Ipswich, when tragically he was diagnosed with non-Hodgkin lymphoma and passed away in 2012 at the age of just 46. The message sent by Everton to Ablett Junior's side talked of how proud his father would have been at his and Warrington Rylands' achievements.

Well-backed financially and having performed well in their league over the last couple of years, Rylands are undoubtedly the favourites, but they look nervy early on. Looking to play a possession game building from the back, goalkeeper Graeme McCall plays an absolute suicide ball instead, and Walsall Wood forward John Atherton is able to nip in to suddenly find himself in on goal. Just as the bloke standing in front of me inside the ground finishes his exclamation of 'oh, for fuck's sake', McCall redeems himself with an instinctive save to divert the ball out for a corner.

Despite this early flash of excitement, Dan is paying virtually no interest in the game, instead glued to his phone, which is propped up against the top of the fence. One hand holding on to the fence for stability, the other grasping an umbrella to shield him, but most importantly his phone, from the continuous drizzling rain. Usually, this sort of behaviour would wind me up, especially given the journey we've made to get there, but today I can't exactly blame him. Dan's phone is showing the live stream of Sutton United's away fixture at Maidenhead United (being played behind closed doors, of course), the third in a run of five games where if we win all five, we will be crowned champions. Ironically, it was our local rivals Bromley who handed us this position of advantage, holding our title rivals Torquay to a 0-0 draw in their own backyard. We won our game in hand against Woking three days later, surviving the most genuinely terrifying last ten minutes ever to win 3-2, meaning we were a point clear and on the home straight. With matters now in our hands, I'm so nervous I can't watch. While Dan keeps a close eye on his phone, I do all I can to try and block it out and focus on the FA Vase semi-final in front of my face. It's not easy.

From what I do successfully manage to watch, the red shirts of Walsall Wood look like they could upset the odds. Managed by former Aston Villa striker and Jamaica international Darren Byfield, they're well-organised and seem happy to let Rylands make a mistake before looking to strike. Having won only four of their ten league games before the season suspension, they could be considered a surprise package to have got this far, but their record in the curtailed 2019/20 season tells you otherwise. Having been well in the title race in what is a tough league, the Midland Football League Premier Division, they'll fancy their chances of getting to Wembley despite being the underdog.

After their early defensive mishap, you'd have thought Warrington would learn somewhat, but 20 minutes in they do more or less exactly the same thing. With a three-on-two situation in the attackers' favour, Wood look certain to score, but again keeper McCall comes out on top. It seems as though the whole visiting team stop and hold their heads in their hands for a second, which gives Rylands all the time they need to break. Andy Scarisbrick gets between the midfield and defence and slots a beautifully weighted pass to the lively Kane Drummond. He displays none of the nerves that have afflicted his defence in the early stages, rounding the keeper and passing coolly into the back of the net to spark wild celebrations from the home faithful, or the few of them that have made it inside the ground anyway. Drummond, a talented teenager formerly of Liverpool's academy side, became the first contracted player in Warrington Rylands' history back in January 2020 amid interest from a series of higher-ranked sides. He certainly looks a good investment now.

After the commotion dies down, there's the distinct echo of a second celebration somewhere in the distance. At first, I think it's some ridiculously tinpot crowd noise piped through the speaker, but it turns out they're actually showing a live stream of the game in the bar adjacent to the ground. It sounds like there must be hundreds of people packed inside, yet maybe only 50 people are allowed inside the actual ground. If the game were to be played two days later, though, when restrictions are due to be eased, then 300 people would be allowed inside Gorsey Lane to watch the game in the flesh, outside and better ventilated.

Mind you, the rules haven't stopped a fair number of like-minded people trying to catch a glimpse of the game however they can. One young lad stands just along from us, peering through a gap in the fence where the tarpaulin lining behind the metal bars has peeled away. It only gives a thin sliver of visibility, though, and given it only allows the lad to view the end the away side are attacking, he soon gives up and looks for entertainment elsewhere, perhaps chancing his arm at getting served across the road in the bar. Faces appear in the flats behind the goal, and in the communal gardens in front of the block a picnic table comes under strain with four well-built blokes stood on it. The long-haired man we met in the pub earlier has made it too, stood on a grass bank just in front of the picnic table between his two shopping bags. It's such a cold day I wouldn't be surprised if he's stocked up on items from the freezer aisle. Every now and then, a local resident walks past and does a double-take when they spot the blokes on the picnic table and the stepladder pushed up against the fence of the ground. The bizarre collection of vantage points gives it a very typical non-league feel.

Having had a few chances in the early stages, conceding the goal knocks the stuffing out of Walsall Wood. More than anything, though, it seems to settle Warrington down more, and they start spraying the ball around without the weight of the world on their shoulders any more. Wood keeper James Wren is unimpressed, his loud shout of 'FUCK ME' reverberating around the local estate after he's called into action to deny Rylands' dynamic number nine, Elliott Nevitt. His team-mates can't exactly miss the message, but they don't really up the intensity and are glad to hear the half-time whistle when it comes. They're not the only ones glad to hear the whistle as the pre-match drinks start to have a substantial effect on my bladder, and the second the referee halts the game I jump down from the stepladder and search for somewhere to relieve myself.

As I sprint off towards the nearest set of semi-hidden bushes, Dan remains in place, still glued to his phone as the live stream of the Sutton game plays out. I've specifically told him not to tell me the score; it's simply too stressful as I try to enjoy the Vase game in front of me, but I can tell from my flat-mate's reaction that it's still a stalemate when only a win will do. It's funny how much he's getting into it, though, and to be honest, it's all my fault. Dan and I met in 2017 at the leaving party of a mutual friend, who was jetting off to Berlin for his university years. We got talking as he had attended a few Sutton games himself, though he was still very much a casual fan and hadn't bothered with the dreary 1-1 draw against Gateshead that afternoon. As it happened, we were both set to attend the University of Warwick from September, and were even studying the same course. Within a year, we'd become such close mates that I managed to convince him to drive to Slough on a Tuesday night for an FA Cup replay that we lost on penalties, and the rest is history.

Now almost as obsessed with Sutton United as me, the tension is starting to get to him. Three more games. That's it. But we need a goal.

To take my mind off it, the Rylands players emerge from the tunnel for the second half, and the game soon gets under way again. Having started the first half somewhat nervously, the home side don't mess about in the second and win a penalty five minutes in. They're attacking towards the end the stepladder is pitched at now, and so I have a perfect view as Ste Milne receives a long ball forward, cuts inside, and is brought down by the Walsall Wood defender. Protestations to the referee from the Wood players are few and far between. The talismanic Elliott Nevitt is tasked with taking the spot-kick. The 24-year-old is having a busy weekend, and has the final of the FA Sunday Cup to play tomorrow for Liverpool-based Campfield against St Joseph's at England's training base, St George's Park. Playing two games on two consecutive days is an impressive feat, but it might not be something that Nevitt can get away with for much longer, as a host of Football League clubs are rumoured to be interested in signing him in the summer.

Given the pedigree of one of non-league football's top marksmen, there's never really any doubt about the outcome of the penalty, and Nevitt thumps it convincingly into the bottom corner to make it 2-0. The goal is scored at the end with the block of flats, the picnic table and the long-haired man from the pub; there are a few celebrations but not everyone looks overly pleased. It's not implausible that some of the spectators actually support the other, traditionally bigger, side in Warrington: Warrington Town. The Yellows play two divisions above Rylands in the Northern Premier League Premier Division, and made national headlines in 2014 when they survived a barrage of pressure to knock League Two side Exeter City out of the FA Cup. Since then, they've gone from strength to strength themselves and if it wasn't for the pandemic they would have been knocking on the door for promotion to National League North. You sense the fear that Rylands might overtake them and achieve the feat before Town themselves manage it.

In fact, Warrington Town reached the FA Vase Final themselves back in 1987 but lost to another local side, St

Helens Town, so should Rylands go one further this year there's an immediate opportunity for one-upmanship. The loud singing coming from the bar after the penalty goes in suggests that the blue side of Warrington firmly believe they can do it. It looks good on the pitch as well and, if truth be told, Walsall Wood now look a beaten side. Rylands push forward, looking for a killer third goal. There are gaps at the back for the visitors as they start to take more risks, and a half-cleared corner comes back into the box for Nevitt to get another strike on goal. The shot ripples the net, but it's the side netting rather than the back of the net that it's struck. Thirty seconds later, another loud celebration arises from the nearby bar, as they clearly don't have an angle on the video that allows them to tell the difference. In the next few minutes, Walsall Wood keeper James Wren makes two good saves as his side cling on to their FA Vase hopes by their fingertips.

All of a sudden, during an injury break, there's a very loud shout from right next to me, and Dan falls off the stepladder and into the brambles below. It doesn't take me long to realise what's going on – Sutton have scored. Sutton have scored! The two of us dance around in giddy jubilation on a patch of brambles in the rain, while everyone else looks on in confusion. This would be massive, enormous, incredible, if we could just hang on. The realisation that we do need to hang on hits me just seconds later, and my joy turns into a sudden overwhelming fear. The shaking of my knees rattles the stepladder as I climb up to watch the rest of the Warrington Rylands game, or at least just try in vain to distract myself as the fate of my beloved local team comes to the forefront of my mind once more. I barely clock what's going on in front of my eyes for the last half-hour, my mind preoccupied with running through every bad thing that might happen over in Berkshire. God, I'm desperate for us to pull this off. We've come too far for it to slip now.

As the minutes tick down, the nerves get worse and worse. Back on the pitch, in front of my eyes, it's still 2-0, and Rylands are still the better side, but I don't really care. My mood depends entirely on the score in the Sutton game; I've only been able to avoid it for so long. I find myself watching the stream on Dan's phone as Sutton's Omar Bugiel gets in down the flank and squares the ball. In what seems like slow motion, Isaac Olaofe meets it and coolly slots home. It's 2-0. IT'S FUCKING TWO-NIL. Again, we celebrate like madmen, almost in tears; we're so nearly there now. Two games and ten minutes away, but it feels like for ever. The sense of foreboding takes over again, and in such a state I ask Dan if he wouldn't mind watching the last ten minutes elsewhere so I can try and take my mind off it. For whatever reason, I'm more than happy to watch under normal circumstances from the stadium itself, but there's something about watching via a stream that I can't stand. It's almost as if I feel as though I have an element of control in being there in the flesh, as though my support can pull the boys through. Up here in Warrington, hundreds of miles away, I'm powerless.

Dan, thankfully, agrees to take his phone round to where the long-haired man from the pub was standing until he bizarrely left just after the second goal. Apparently, he lives in Nantwich, a town less than 30 miles away, but the last bus from Warrington town centre leaves just after 5pm and he didn't want to miss it. I'll never moan about the District line in London again.

Now Dan and the Sutton live stream are out of the way, I try to focus my attention back towards the FA Vase tie in front of my face. It kicked off before the Sutton game, and so is inside the last five minutes as Rylands edge closer and closer to a historic day out at Wembley. Further along from where our stepladder is set up, a young girl balances on her father's shoulders, searching for a glimpse of the glory that is now surely set to unfold. Clearly excited, she wears a grin from ear to ear, and her father doesn't seem at all bothered by the fact he's sacrificing his own view so his daughter can get a sight of history unfolding at the humble surroundings of Gorsey Lane. It's a wonderful view of just what it means to people, of the simple joys supporting your local team can bring. I doubt many things can beat watching your local side at Wembley, and they're in touching distance now, minutes away. As I stand there and take in the unbridled joy of the collection of characters around me, Walsall Wood score.

It's an absolutely fantastic goal as well, to be fair. A bit of neat interplay gets the ball to substitute Tom Hawks, who hits it first time from more than 25 yards out. You can see his thought process, given there's less than five minutes to go and his side have barely managed a shot since going behind, but even Hawks himself looks a little surprised when the ball sails into the top corner. Having been dead and buried, all of a sudden there's life in Walsall Wood once more. Sadly, there's life in the overactive pessimistic side of my brain too. Warrington Rylands couldn't have been more comfortable at 2-0, yet now find themselves hanging on for dear life, having led by two goals into stoppage time.

I don't know what's been happening over in Maidenhead, but the visitors' goal here makes the possibility that we might let our own lead slip very real in my mind. My knees start shaking again, my stomach is churning, my mind all over the place. In five minutes or so, it will all be over, and hopefully I'll be able to celebrate with a drink or two back in town. I won't be the only one doing so if Rylands can hold on to their own lead here.

Walsall Wood aren't giving up without a fight, and pile everyone forward for a long throw. The girl on her dad's shoulders is probably barely old enough to comprehend what is going on, but her expression has still changed as she picks up the nerves of everyone else around. The only noise as the ball is launched into the box comes from the encouragement of the handful of Wood officials who have been allowed into Gorsey Lane, with the rest of the stadium being held in a deathly silence. The ball receives a flick-on, and arcs towards the far post. There are bodies in red there to attack it too, but it's a Rylands player who gets to the ball first and clears. Everyone breathes once more. It's all the away side have time for too, and the whistle goes seconds afterwards. Warrington Rylands have done it; they'll be at Wembley next week for the FA Vase Final.

For a moment or two, I allow myself to enjoy the celebrations of the home side, who have been on quite a journey in the last few years. As you'd expect, the squad and management team are over the moon, dancing around the centre circle and singing about their illustrious destination next week as their opponents collapse to the turf, dejected, broken. I don't dare to check the Sutton score yet, instead wondering which of the two sides I'll resemble in a few minutes when the full-time score comes in. Out of the corner of my eye, I catch Dan sprinting round the corner, with a look that could have come straight from the faces of one of the players in blue, the winning side from today's semi-final.

'It's 3-0!' he screams at me from barely a yard away when he reaches the stepladder. 'Louis John has scored from his own half!'

You'd be forgiven for thinking we were watching the Rylands game on the delayed stream they have on in the bar as we embrace in joyous laughter, basking in the magnificence of our unfancied local side. It's a different local side to the one everyone around us is celebrating, of course, but who cares? To get to Wembley is an incredible achievement for any ninth-tier side, but the underdog story I truly yearn for is the part-timers of Sutton United beating the likes of Notts County and Stockport to win promotion to the Football League for the first time. We're now just two games away. Two horrible, stressful, terrifying, potentially glorious games. That's it.

It's amazing how much the result of a football match can lift your mood in the middle of such a strange time. Warrington Rylands have pulled off the greatest moment in their history, yet barely anyone has been able to see it. That's not going to stop those who watched on the live stream, via online updates, or over the fence, from partying all night, though. Similarly, Sutton United are on the verge of football's biggest underdog story since Leicester City won the Premier League. Fans have been present at just two games all season, one of which we lost, yet if we do pull it off, it will change people's lives for ever. It's almost illogical, and downright bizarre, but that's football for you. For many people, it's been the only positive in a year of lockdown-induced misery. More than ever, it's shown just how important the sport is.

Our train home doesn't depart for three hours, a money-saving strategy that allows Dan and me to spend any potential savings and more in a pub in town while we wait. We settle on the Barley Mow, an old-fashioned boozer just past the wonderfully named Cockhedge Shopping Centre, still enjoying the fact that we can get a pint for less than a fiver now we're not in London. Golden Square in the centre of Warrington exists entirely independently of the microcosm of Gorsey Lane, and you would get no hint of Rylands' recent triumph even if you spent all night there. It feels distinctly middle-class, with colourful bunting adorning the Old Fish Market shelter and artisan shops facing out into the square. The punters at the various bars dotted around are all either smartly dressed or clad in the blue and yellow of Warrington Wolves.

Rylands might be the second-biggest football club in Warrington, but even the two football clubs together would have nothing on Warrington Wolves in terms of support. The rugby league club dominate, and every replica kit you see is one of theirs, even though they don't play until Monday night. A local area where rugby is the main sport is as alien to Dan and me as the whole lockdown thing was back last March, and we're happy to keep ourselves to ourselves, the only item on the agenda being Sutton United's fantastic win today. As good as this season has been, the situation with various lockdowns has meant we've never really had the chance to celebrate and drink in the result after a win. Still walking on air, neither of us wants the night to end.

Time runs its inevitable course, though, and before we know it, we're whisked back to reality; another week of work coming up with only the football at the end of it to break the monotony. For Warrington Rylands 1906, there's a visit to Wembley next Saturday to look forward to, a spectacle which their supporters will actually be able to attend too. For Dan, myself and the rest of the Sutton United faithful, there's the potential for a first-ever promotion to the Football League lying just around the corner. In both worlds, it is the beautiful game that provides a beam of light in what has otherwise been a year and a half of nothing but darkness. As we walk back to the train station to head home, there's a scene that perfectly encapsulates it: a busker playing the accordion to an empty square.

11

The Final

22 May 2021

THIS IS it. The 612 entrants of the 2020/21 FA Vase have been whittled down to just two. There have been 5-5 thrillers, red cards, penalty shoot-out dramas, all amid the backdrop of pandemic uncertainty, meaning there were stages where nobody knew if the competition was ever going to reach a finish at all. It has done, though, and as usual, what a finish it will be. For the players, staff, volunteers and supporters of Binfield and Warrington Rylands, it will be a once-in-a-lifetime opportunity to take their usual role and perform it at Wembley Stadium for the day. Crucially, for the first time in the second half of the competition, and indeed in the calendar year, supporters will be allowed to attend the match.

With the schedule and rules since Christmas meaning I've had to watch games as either a cameraman or shady bloke peering over the fence, you'd like to think that switching the venue to a stadium capable of holding 90,000 people would make my life a little bit easier. Wrong. Almost unbelievably, it is announced that each team will only be allowed 1,500 tickets, a move that seems to be taking caution to an extreme. Exactly a week earlier, the day Rylands booked their final spot by beating Walsall Wood, the FA Cup Final between Chelsea and Leicester City had been played in front of 20,000 at the same stadium. Less than two months later, the final of Euro 2020 is set to take place, with the stadium at a much greater capacity. It doesn't seem too much to allow everyone from Warrington and Binfield who wants to attend this momentous occasion to do so, but nobody is changing their minds anytime soon. It's going to have to do.

Given that you can't exactly watch over the fence at Wembley, I'm going to have to find a ticket somehow if I want to complete my unique 'road to Wembley' in the FA Vase this season. Binfield, having secured their final place a week earlier than Rylands, announce their plan for ticket sales straight away. It's not good news. They're only selling tickets in person at the club bar in the small Berkshire village, with none of their sales online. I can understand why, to be fair – with such a small number of tickets available, they want to make sure any locals with even a vague interest in the club get a chance to attend. The policy is designed to keep out those with no connection to the side, and I expect Warrington Rylands will probably do the same. I'm very much staring down the barrel of the poor-ticket-allocation-at-Wembley gun.

I've gone too far on this journey to give up now, though, and come up with a plan. My work hours are flexible, meaning that if I wake up at five o'clock in the morning and start half an hour later, I can clock off at around three in the afternoon, and head over to Binfield on public transport in time for their club bar opening two and a half hours later. I'd pop in, buy two tickets, and then instantly turn around and begin my two-and-a-half-hour return journey. The ground itself is in the middle of absolutely nowhere too, only really reachable by car, and I'd have to walk for half an hour down an unlit country lane with no pavement to get there. It's absolutely ridiculous, but given the way the world is at the moment, this doesn't come as a particular surprise any more.

Halfway into my work day, about six coffees and three Red Bulls in, a message pops up on the Warrington Rylands Twitter account. They're planning to sell tickets for their end via the phone, which would save me my daft journey later on. I call them up in a state of nervy optimism, having previously already resigned myself to my trip to Binfield. The woman on the other end tells me they're not in fact selling tickets over the phone but will set up an online portal later today. Do I believe her? I suspect my obvious London accent might have put them off selling to me, so I give Louis from the Malvern game a text and tell him to call up and pretend to be Scouse. An accent master, he does as he's told but still gets nowhere. I don't attempt to call up again masquerading as a Mancunian just in case. The clock ticks down to three, and still there's no sign of tickets online. It's hard to express just how much I can't be arsed to go to Binfield at this point, but I simply need to get tickets.

I'm desperate for this trip to Wembley now, but it could all have been so different. The Sutton United title race is still in full swing; in fact, we're almost scarily close now. The day after our victory against Maidenhead, Torquay slipped up again with a 2-2 draw against Stockport County. Our lead at the top of the table with two games to go stands at three points, and with fans now allowed back into stadiums, I'm desperate to be there as we chase the final few points we need to get across the line. Our penultimate game, at home to Hartlepool, has blissfully been moved to Sunday for live TV coverage. Had it been scheduled for the Saturday, as is virtually every other game in the National League, I'd have had to have given the FA Vase Final a miss.

Ready to leave my Aldgate apartment, still a complete zombie, I take one last look at the Twitter page for Warrington Rylands. Hang on a second. Yes, it's there! Feeling like I've just won the lottery, I get on to the portal, purchase the tickets I need, and collapse into my bed. In saving me my budget magical mystery tour, Warrington Rylands have just earned my undying affection. I could cry with joy as I think of all the public transport pain I've been spared. Three trains, a bus, and then a potentially life-threatening walk didn't sound like much fun to me. I don't fancy getting killed before Sutton win the league.

Taking a while to recover from my five o'clock start, work for the rest of the week is about as much fun as watching Sutton defend a long throw-in when a goal ahead in stoppage time, but there's the promise of a great weekend of football at the end of it. Visits to Wembley are always a great occasion, no matter who's playing there. Growing up playing football virtually every day, 'Wembley' was always the main playground game going. Split into either doubles or singles, it was a pretty simple concept to grasp. There would be one goalkeeper in one goal, with everyone out on the pitch aiming to score. If you did net, you were through.

The last one to do so would be out. This would repeat, round by round, until you had a winner, though I would typically be out long before this point.

I can remember one particular 'Wembley Singles' injustice, in which I reached the final in year two of primary school. Looking to pull off a shock on the scale of Greece's Euro 2004 win a few years earlier, I got the first goal in a best-of-three final, needing only one more to take an unlikely title and bragging rights until morning break the next day. In a scramble, the sponge ball broke to my opponent, who hammered it towards goal, right at the bottom corner. Without even thinking about the fact we were playing on concrete, and not trusting the goalkeeper, who was only there because he couldn't play football himself, I flung myself to the ground and stopped the ball with my chest, keeping my arm tucked behind my back. The watching crowd assumed I had handballed it, such was the majesty of the block, and gave my opponent a goal despite my furious protestations. Downhearted by this, and hampered by the fact my left arm was completely numb from having slammed it into the concrete floor, my final dreams were effectively over, and I returned to early-round obscurity for the rest of my school days.

Despite obsessively competing in 'Wembley' from a young age, I never actually visited the national stadium until the London Olympics in 2012. It was a bit of a random choice, Senegal vs Mexico in the quarter-finals, but up in the gods in the top tier we witnessed a fantastic game as the Senegalese, spearheaded by a young Sadio Mané, fought back from two goals down to force extra time. Mexico were too strong in the end, and went on to win the tournament, but I remember being mesmerised by the atmosphere in the stadium even though the majority of the 80,000-strong crowd couldn't care less who won. In more recent years, I've been back several times, mostly for FA Vase finals where you can get tickets for the comfy padded seats for the price of a few London pints. The one thing that I've always yearned for, though, still remains elusive. I would die to see Sutton United play at Wembley. In the summer of 2018, we reached the National League play-off semi-final, needing just one win in a home game against Boreham Wood to reach the final at Wembley. We lost 3-2, and I still haven't really got over it. If we did manage to get to the Football League by winning the title instead, though, I think I'd happily let it slide for a while.

Despite his unfortunate failure to win over the Warrington Rylands ticket saleswoman with his Scouse accent over the phone, Louis is joining me for the FA Vase Final. Indeed, he's staying over all weekend, with a ticket to Sutton's vital clash against Hartlepool on the Sunday too. With his parents now vaccinated, it's the first time he's been on a weekend away anywhere since our fateful trip to Croatia back in August, where we'd managed to catch coronavirus in a country where there were supposedly only around 200 new cases a day. Understandably, his clinically vulnerable parents haven't been quite so keen for him to get out and about since then, though at least they didn't catch anything on that occasion. The country is still far from out of the woods with this pandemic, but at least the vaccination programme is offering some hope of normal life returning soon. My good friend from university has landed a job down in London, starting in September, so is due to move down and join me in the capital then. The hope is that with many of my mates together, and the vaccine rollout paving the way for some normality to return, we can make up for lost time from then. It's so close but still teasing, out of reach for now.

Of all the FA Vase games I've trekked to this season, Wembley is by far the easiest one to get to. The Metropolitan line takes us straight there, and unlike a typical Wembley day out, there are no real crowds. With such a low number of fans allowed to attend, you would hardly be able to tell there was an event on at all as the train pulls into Wembley Park with only two or three other people in our carriage. It's barely an hour until kick-off.

Without the collective buzz of a large crowd, you can pick up on all the idiosyncrasies of those lucky enough to have got tickets. The highlight is four lads, very much worse for wear, butchering one of Joy Division's all-time greats with the lyrics 'Rylands, tearing Cockneys apart again'. On their run to the final, Rylands haven't played a single side within 100 miles of London, and even Binfield is a good way outside the M25, closer to Reading and Oxford than the East End. Clearly, none of the group have been tearing geography lessons apart recently. There are a few police officers walking around, and one Warrington fan asked, 'Have you got any spare tickets, Officer? Not a parking ticket,' before bursting into loud laughter at his own joke. The officers look more likely to arrest him than join in with his glee, walking off stony-faced as everyone around looks at each other as if to say, 'Miserable twats.'

I'm a bit of a miserable twat myself once I get into the ground, as I'm charged £2.60 for a small bottle of water. We're at least near one of the water refill machines, and I make a mental note to top up as much as I can to get my money's worth. Louis doesn't even go as far as purchasing a bottle of water, and says that on principle he'd rather sit there in the summer heat and dehydrate for hours than pay the money being asked of him. When the concourse gets quiet, he puts his head under the water machine and takes on what fluid he can, lapping the odd drop up with his tongue like a very frugal cat. The array of images behind the food and drink stalls acts almost as an attempt to justify the exorbitant pricing. 'Yes, we might charge stupid money for a drink but Geoff Hurst won us the World Cup here 55 years ago, so put up or shut up.'

The bottled water prices are soon forgotten about as we head out into the stands, to find our seats and get a view of the Wembley pitch for the first time in a while. For Louis, it's his first visit to the iconic stadium, a fact that shocks me as much as it makes me laugh. I thought Senegal vs Mexico in the Olympics was an odd first Wembley game, but it's not quite Binfield vs Warrington Rylands in front of a crowd barely larger than the queue for a good London fish and chip shop. It might not feel like a big occasion to the outsider, though, but I'm still very much looking forward to it, and Louis too has had a strong interest in the competition since witnessing the 5-5 draw at Malvern back in December. I can only imagine how special it must be for the 1,500 fans from each side, not to mention the players actually getting to play on the hallowed turf. Every football fan's fantasy, most will assume you lose the chance to do it as soon as you're not going to make it as a top-level professional player. The FA Vase is a beautiful back route, a scenic route, to childhood dreams.

There might not be many people in the ground, but there's still the unmistakeable roar of emotional encouragement, of pride and hope, as the players come out of the tunnel. It makes me almost nostalgic; it's been so long since I've been inside a football ground with a crowd in attendance. Everyone is situated in the lower tier on the same side of the ground, with the Binfield section to the left-hand side and the Warrington Rylands end, the end I'm in, on the right. Social distancing rules mean nobody can sit together, but the crowd being spread out makes it seem a lot larger than just 3,000. Some of the players look for family in the crowd as they take their positions, giving a big grin and a wave when they spot them. The FA Vase Final is to be followed by the FA Trophy equivalent, some four hours after the Vase kick-off, and there are a couple of fans of the sides competing in that, Hereford and Hornchurch, dotted around on the other side of the ground. One lone man behind the goal in the Hornchurch end, a solitary figure in a cavernous, empty stadium, watches on as Binfield get us under way in the final of the strangest FA Vase campaign ever seen.

Meanwhile, my phone is turned off as I attempt to focus fully on the game in front of my face, rather than events elsewhere. Though Sutton don't play until tomorrow, our title rivals Torquay play today at home to bottom club Barnet. A heavy win for them would move them ahead of us on goal difference, and really heap the pressure on ahead of tomorrow. On the other hand, if you're much more of an optimist than I am, any dropped points against the division's basement club will mean we can secure the title with a win against Hartlepool. It's not a thought my mind can handle at this point, so I choose to stay well away from it for now. At any rate, while the FA Vase game kicks off just after midday, the Torquay match isn't until three o'clock. There's a long way to go before we discover our fate yet.

Back at Wembley and away from the endless National League permutations running through my mind, Binfield and Warrington Rylands both look lively early on, and it's understandable if they have something of a spring in their step. It was announced on the Tuesday building up to the game that the FA would alter the non-league pyramid slightly, in doing so promoting some of the sides who had been at the top of their leagues over the last couple of Covid-hit seasons. Both Warrington Rylands and Binfield were among those teams rewarded for their success, taking them both to the highest level in their histories. Victory today for either side would complete a unique double success. As the two teams settle down into the game, the crowd settles down slightly too, so you can hear every shout of the players on the pitch. 'Lino, he's fucking caught that!' screams one of the Warrington centre-backs after a Binfield player takes the ball down on his chest and looks to attack. It comes to nothing, and any hard feelings between defender and match official are soon forgotten, but the comedy value of having such a typical non-league atmosphere at Wembley Stadium isn't lost on anyone.

Binfield win a free kick out wide, and the ball is whipped into the box by Kensley Maloney. Rylands can't seem to get it away, and there's an almighty scramble before it falls to captain Sean Moore in the box. It's only at his feet for a fraction of a second, but he gets a good strike off. Sadly, it goes just the wrong side of the bar and ends up being more of a threat to the lone Hornchurch fan than Rylands keeper Graeme McCall. The Hellenic League side remain on top in the early stages, and Moore is a constant threat. As has been a recurring theme in FA Vase finals in recent years, the quality of football is good, surprising those who don't already know and appreciate just how entertaining and skilful the ninth tier of English football can be. The large Wembley pitch feeds that further, preventing the match becoming a war of attrition over a game of football. The crowd start to get into it more and more, and pockets of chanting break out among some of the younger fans in the crowd. Before long, the two most vocal groups on each side are gesturing and shouting abuse at each other. If teenage football fans shouting witless insults and making wanker gestures across a segregation fence isn't a sure sign that football is back, then I don't know what is.

Around 20 minutes into the game, Rylands start to get more of a foothold in the game and look more likely. Rick Smith, a centre-back who only recently joined the club on a dual-registration deal from higher-ranked Atherton Collieries, plays a delightful ball forward, and all of a sudden Ste Milne is in. As easy as you like, he rounds goalkeeper Chris Grace to put his side in front. The celebrations don't last, though, as gradually the supporters around me spot the linesman with his flag up on the far side. While joy turns to despair, the change in moods is the other way round in the Binfield end, and the gesticulation across the segregation line continues. By this point, a group of fans on each side have actually moved over specifically with the intention of shouting abuse at each other. The stewards, who had previously stopped Louis and me from sitting next to each other as a result of social distancing laws, do nothing.

Two minutes later, Rylands have the ball in the net again, and this time it counts. Now free of inhibitions, the end around me erupts as the whole team run towards the supporters to celebrate. The Binfield fans who minutes ago had been mocking their Rylands counterparts quickly fade away back to their seats, trying to limit the embarrassment as much as possible. The goalscorer, surprise surprise, is Elliott Nevitt. The day after his goal in the semi-final success, Nevitt scored an extra-time winner in the FA Sunday Cup for Campfield. Very much like his team as a whole, he's hoping to complete a unique double, and is certainly going the right way about it so far.

There's a real buzz in the Rylands end now as their side start to zip the ball about on the pristine Wembley surface, looking more and more confident by the second. Much like the Walsall Wood game, they've reacted perfectly to going ahead – they say you're at your most vulnerable when you score, but not Warrington Rylands. The Merseyside club burst forward again, and Milne picks out his strike-partner Nevitt with a perfectly weighted ball. Through on goal and onside, Nevitt shapes to shoot and get his second of the afternoon, but out of nowhere Binfield defender Liam Gavin gets across and makes the block. Some of the fans around me can't believe it; they seemed so sure that their star man would tuck that away and put the game almost beyond Binfield at an early stage. The ball breaks away and is cleared down the left-hand side of the pitch, where it's picked up by Binfield's Sean Moore. It's all too easy and he drops his shoulder, gets to the byline and puts the ball into the box. Liam Ferdinand doesn't connect with the header properly, but from only a yard or two out it doesn't matter, and the ball ends up in the back of the net anyway. It's 1-1.

The instant change of moods in both ends is incredible. From feeling like they were dominating and pushing on for a killer second, a deathly silence drops over the Rylands end as everyone mentally replays that missed chance just 30 seconds earlier. The nerves among the Binfield supporters as they came under the cosh are replaced with a newfound energy, a belief that the momentum is behind them now. The kids giving it large across the segregation fence return with a vengeance, but the fans they're shouting at look dumbstruck more than angry. If we didn't before, we certainly have a game on our hands now.

Celebrations and verbal exchanges are still very much ongoing as Rylands kick off and play the ball forward into the channel. Warrington winger Charlie Doyle chasing it is quick, quicker than Liam Gavin is expecting, and as they both reach the penalty area, he gets a toe to the ball as Gavin slides in. Gavin's boot can only make contact with where the ball was, now the location of Doyle's shin, and the referee has no hesitation in pointing to the spot. Having been a goal-saving hero with his block barely a minute ago, Gavin is now the villain. If the emotions in the stands were quick to change, I can only imagine what's going through his mind now. It's Nevitt to take the penalty, against Binfield's own penalty hero of previous rounds in Chris Grace. Grace goes the right way, but the spot-kick is so perfectly placed in the corner that he has no chance. It's all change again. There's still time for Binfield to have a corner cleared off the line before the whistle goes for half-time, sadly bringing to an end a sensational half of football.

The half-time big-screen presenter stands right in front of our seats in the front row, going back over some of the highlights of an action-packed first half. It's quite nice to be able to catch your breath and fully take in what's been going on, with the highlights being shown on the big screen not a benefit you're likely to get at either club's home ground. A message of 'please respect your fellow fans' over the Tannoy is met with boos from the two sets of vocal supporters, causing the rest of the stadium to have a little chuckle. It's all good-natured, injecting further life into a sport that relies on its supporters for so much of its entertainment value. It really is nice to have everyone back and not have to watch over a fence or through a camera lens.

The second half starts slowly, as if both sides are trying to get a feel of each other all over again. The style is very non-committal, very measured, and neither team wants to give anything away. Binfield aren't too gung-ho yet, but then Warrington Rylands aren't sitting back, either. Though currently in the position of strength, they know that it would only take one slip-up, one mistake, for it all to change again. You can sense the crowd getting more nervy as the seconds tick by, with the volume of the singing dropping, replaced by evermore-frequent oohs and aahs every time the ball goes near the penalty area. The shouts of the players, too, start to feel more on edge, more cautious of what might happen rather than hopeful of what they could make happen. The next goal is absolutely crucial.

Not a lot happens until Rylands get a corner around the hour mark. It's whipped in, the defending is statuesque, and Elliott Nevitt finds himself between two defenders. He's not going to miss, and his goal sparks raptures in the seats around me. Nevitt is clearly ecstatic: a Wembley hat-trick isn't something many people can tick off their bucket list. It's the first hat-trick anyone has scored at Wembley since Harry Kane against Montenegro in England's 1,000th international, in 2019, and the first in an FA Vase Final at the new Wembley Stadium. In fact, in getting his third goal, Nevitt registered only the second hat-trick ever in an FA Vase Final, with the first coming from Doug Young of Billericay against the wonderfully named Almondsbury Greenway in 1979.

With the scoreline now at 3-1, being non-committal and measured isn't going to do Binfield any good. They've got to go for it. Their supporters look beaten, though, stunned into silence by Nevitt's incredible hat-trick, and all the noise is from those in the end where Louis and I are sitting. Counting down to victory, they gloat and sing the praises of those wearing blue on the Wembley turf in equal measure. Many of the supporters in the ground are family members of those on the pitch, and there are a lot of proud-looking faces around me. Any nervousness that exists among the Rylands contingent is in them, desperate to see their sons, brothers, fathers, cousins, uncles, nephews, boyfriends, husbands be victorious at Wembley. The vocal group, dressed almost exclusively in Stone Island attire, seem less concerned. In their heads, the trophy is already on its way back to Warrington.

Binfield aren't giving up just yet, though, and a wicked in-swinging cross finds Oliver Harris free, only six yards from goal. Keeper McCall is quick off his line, though, and able to make the block, but the ball falls to Sean Moore. His header loops towards goal, with McCall still on the ground, but his defenders come to the rescue to clear off the line. There's life in the Berkshire side yet.

Another looping cross comes into the box, but it's hopeful and easily cleared to safety. The ball is recycled to Liam Ferdinand, who stands more or less on his own, with three defenders around him. I look to the big screen to check how long is left, and when I look back, the ball is in the back of the net and the Binfield supporters are celebrating wildly. Quite how he's managed to do that, I have no idea. The shot didn't look on at all, never mind scoring it. The clock reads 67 minutes as the goal goes in; there's still plenty of time for another as the side in red rush the ball back to the centre spot to seek an equaliser. In the blink of an eye, the mood has changed once more. It feels like a completely different game to the one I was watching just seconds earlier, with the Warrington fans now silent and their Binfield counterparts in full voice, having found renewed hope. 'COME ON, BINFIELD. COME ON, BINFIELD' rings out from virtually the entire end, 1,500 voices roaring their side on. I might be in the Rylands end, but I hope they do get an equaliser, just to see the scenes that would ensue. I've missed that sort of thing over the last year and a half.

Responding to the crowd, Binfield get well on top and really push for a goal. In turn, the crowd get louder, feeding off each other in a virtuous cycle for them but a vicious one for Rylands, who find themselves penned in, unable to relieve the pressure. After a period camped in the Rylands half, a deep cross after a half-cleared corner picks out Liam Ferdinand at the far post. On a hat-trick himself, he gets his head to the ball, but it goes agonisingly wide of the far post. Two Wembley hat-tricks in the same game would truly be a remarkable story, but time starts to run out and it looks less and less likely as Rylands get a stranglehold of the game once more. Regaining their composure, they suck the life out of the mini Binfield revival and look to counter when their opponents are still reeling from another attack breaking down. Nevitt, a constant pain in the arse for the opposing defenders, gets in down the channel and pulls a ball across for wonderkid Kane Drummond. He takes a touch and sets himself, but by the time he gets the ball out of his feet, Binfield keeper Chris Grace is out to make the block. It's a golden chance to kill the game off with 15 minutes to go, and Drummond can scarcely believe he's missed it.

It doesn't look like it will matter, though. Binfield look exhausted, dead on their feet, and the noise to the left of me has died down. It's never going to be exactly comfortable with a single-goal lead in a cup final, but Rylands see out the final few minutes with minimal threat. In fact, Nevitt gets through on goal and really should get his fourth, but a good save from Grace denies him seconds before the full-time whistle goes. That's it.

The Binfield players sink to the ground, but only for a few seconds and they head over to the stands to speak to their friends and family, determined to treasure the occasion despite the result. There are tears in both camps, and on my side of the segregation fence, the tears are of joy, elation, pride. One lone supporter jumps the fence, runs on to the pitch, does a lap of the penalty box and then evades security as he leaps back over the metal fence and into the seated area to loud cheers from his mates. I don't think a lot of the players' families even realise it's happening. Someone pushes past me with a thick Scouse accent, apologising and introducing himself as Elliott Nevitt's brother. Carrying a small child, he hands him over to Nevitt to carry across the pitch as he's unsurprisingly named man of the match. Nobody is in a rush to leave as the trophy is lifted, Warrington Rylands writing their name in the history books as the winners of a historic FA Vase campaign.

Just like that, it's over. It started on a Friday night up in County Durham, a chance to briefly get out of the house and take my mind off all that was going on around me. There was a trip down to Bournemouth to catch up with mates I'd barely seen because of the sudden lockdown, a poignant return to university and the tough times I'd experienced, and then a visit to the stadium of the team I love so dearly but have been unable to watch in the flesh since March 2020. The 5-5 thriller up in the scenic Malvern Hills was arguably the highlight of the run, a weekend which preceded another hard lockdown that nobody had seen coming. Coming out the other side brought new challenges, but it was a pleasure to revisit my childhood years of running Fox in the Box Productions through games at Sutton Common Rovers and Hadley. The quarters and semis were completed with some slightly daft watching over the fence, before the Wembley showpiece offered a bizarre replica of the real world. I'd always wanted to do a 'road to Wembley' in the FA Vase, but I never envisaged it going quite like this.

As we sit in a virtually empty stadium and wait for the FA Trophy Final to come around, I can't help but hope and pray that this is the last time in my life I have such a weird experience of football, at times a dystopian experience of football. This sport needs supporters, and misses them as much as they miss football. I could cry at not being able to watch Sutton this season, and there are hundreds of thousands like me pining for their teams across the country, across the world. Getting fans back into Wembley at all, despite the low numbers, is a positive step, the beginning of a long path that will take us back to what we love. If nothing else, the last year or so has made me so much more grateful for what I have. Slightly teary, I drift off into my own little world and reminisce, but also dream of what the future holds.

Tomorrow shines through, but today isn't over yet. As a thrilling Trophy final between Hereford and Hornchurch reaches half-time, I become acutely aware that the Torquay game will have finished by now. Louis asks if I would like to hear the score, and although my head is screaming at me not to let it ruin my day, I simply have to know. 'It was 8-0 Torquay, mate,' Louis says with a grimace. 'Torquay are top.'

Fuck. Oh shit. We need a result tomorrow now, and Hartlepool are chasing the play-offs themselves. Just as I start to panic, I spot a smirk growing on my friend's face. Wondering what the hell is going on, I'm stunned into complete stasis as he turns his phone around and shows me an image that could change my life for ever. It wasn't 8-0 at all. It was a 2-2 draw. Win tomorrow, and against all the odds Sutton United will be champions of the National League. We'll be playing in League Two next season. We're not there yet, of course, but it feels unreal, like a dream. Burying my face in my hands as the tears start to flow, I try, and fail, to take it all in. We're one game from somewhere my home team has never been before, and if we do manage it, I'll be there to see it in the flesh after many long and painful months away. It feels like the perfect way to start a new chapter.

Epilogue

ON SUNDAY, 23 May 2021, *Sutton United* beat Hartlepool 3-0 to secure promotion to the Football League for the first time. The club had asked for my services as a Covid-compliant ball boy for the game, as they had several times already that season, so I decided I was going to try and be fairly professional and not get too emotional, whatever the outcome. I managed to hold it together pretty well until after the full-time whistle, when I joined the players in acknowledging the fans behind the goal. As I forgot all the rules and went to hug my mates on the other side of the pitchside barrier, Dan included, I cried and cried and cried.

We enjoyed three years in the Football League, including a Wembley final in the EFL Trophy in year one, before being relegated back to the National League in 2024. Heartbroken as I was, I'm still a regular match-going fan, and the community spirit remains as strong as ever.

Things have not got any better for *Durham City* since 2020. They were spared relegation in 2020/21 with the season being curtailed early because of lockdown restrictions, but there was no escaping next time. They endured a miserable 2021/22, picking up five points all season with results including three 10-0 defeats and a

16-1 hammering at Carlisle City. Having been relegated into Division One of the Wearside League, they promptly finished bottom of that too, and now play in the Wearside League's second tier alongside the likes of Barnard Castle FC and the perhaps confrontationally named New Durham AFC. *Thackley AFC* are, unsurprisingly, still plying their trade in the same division, for the 42nd year running now. It might not be overly exciting, but no doubt Durham City fans would kill for their consistency.

Whitley Bay, Newcastle University, Bournemouth FC (Poppies) and *Blackfield & Langley* too are all still in the same division at time of writing as they were when I visited them. There's been a bit more excitement over at *Coventry Sphinx*, who won the United Counties League Premier Division South in 2023, earning them promotion to the eighth-tier Northern Premier League Division One Midlands. This puts them unarguably above city rivals Coventry United in the local pecking order, much to my annoyance. The angry man now has a higher standard of opponent to shout at, and with no hard feelings I hope he's having the time of his life. The opponents from their tie, *Heanor Town*, were promoted to the United Counties League Premier Division North in 2021. This came as a result of a non-league restructure which saw some teams promoted based on points per game across all matches over the incomplete 2019/20 and 2020/21 seasons.

Sutton Common Rovers were another beneficiary of this rule in 2021, earning promotion to the Isthmian League South Central Division where they remain today. *Southall* won promotion to the same division a year later by finishing runners-up in the Combined Counties League Premier

Division North. *Malvern* have gone one better, earning promotion through the league restructure in 2021 before following that up with a play-off victory to earn a second consecutive promotion the next season. They now play in the eighth-tier Southern League Division One South. *Sporting Khalsa* also now play in the eighth tier, in the Northern Premier League Division One Midlands, having been one of the 2021 restructure beneficiaries.

Continuing the theme, *Hadley* are now part of the eighth-tier Southern League Division One Central, having been promoted to the division in 2022. *US Portsmouth* were another restructure beneficiary in 2021 but have since been relegated back to the Wessex League Division One. *Flackwell Heath* too have been promoted since the lockdown era, but much more recently, having won the Combined Counties League Premier Division North in 2024. *Walsall Wood* too made the step up to the eighth tier after winning the Midland Football League Premier Division in 2023. Sadly, they resigned from this league due to cost pressures in October 2024 and so their men's first team are in the football wilderness at time of writing.

Both 2020/21 FA Vase finalists have gone on to bigger and better things since their big day out. *Binfield* were another restructure beneficiary and have defended their eighth-tier status since 2021, but the big winners since the days of lockdown have been *Warrington Rylands*. Having been promoted in 2021 due to the restructure (a bit repetitive now, I know), they went on to win the Northern Premier League Division One West at the first time of asking, rising to the Northern Premier League Premier Division. Since then, they haven't quite been able to make National League

North but have been knocking on the door. Stars of the FA Vase run Kane Drummond and Elliott Nevitt moved on to the Football League with Chesterfield and Tranmere Rovers respectively.

* * *

Grandad passed away in June 2021. It was a strange, horrible feeling hearing the news – the typical grief mixed with a feeling of relief that he was no longer suffering. As the man said himself, he'd had a great life. I went up to visit him shortly before he died, when England were playing their Euro 2020 warm-up games at Middlesbrough's Riverside Stadium. As someone who follows England home and away, it felt like a sign to choose that moment to time my visit. The nuances of the football schedule meant I happened to say my goodbyes at the right time. More than ever, I felt like the game had my back.